# Miracles of Jesus

# Miracles of Jesus

Richard S. Ascough

NOVALIS

© 2003 Novalis, Saint Paul University, Ottawa, Canada

Cover: Allegro 168 Inc.

Layout: Richard Proulx

Business Office:
Novalis
49 Front Street East, 2nd Floor
Toronto, Ontario, Canada
M5E 1B3
Phone: 1-877-702-7773 or (416) 363-3303
Fax: 1-877-702-7775 or (416) 363-9409
E-mail: cservice@novalis.ca

www.novalis.ca

National Library of Canada Cataloguing in Publication

Ascough, Richard S. (Richard Stephen)

    Miracles of Jesus / Richard S. Ascough.

    ISBN 2-89507-408-9

    1. Jesus Christ–Miracles.  I. Title.

BT366.3.A73 2003       232.9'55         C2003-903875-0

Printed in Canada.

We acknowledge the financial support of the Government of Canada through the Book Publishing Industry Development Program (BPIDP) for our publishing activities.

5  4  3  2  1       07  06  05  04  03

NOVALIS

*For my parents*
*Beatrice and Michael Ascough*
*and*
*my parents-in-law*
*Helen and Harold Riley*

# Contents

Acknowledgments ............................................... 10

Introduction (by John L. McLaughlin) ...................... 11

1. Jesus the Miracle Worker: "He cured many
   who were sick."
   (Mark 1:32-34) ......................................... 19

2. The Synagogue Demoniac: "I know
   who you are."
   (Mark 1:21-28) ......................................... 24

3. Simon Peter's Mother-in-Law: "She began
   to serve them."
   (Mark 1:29-31) ......................................... 29

4. A Man with Leprosy: "If you choose, you can
   make me clean."
   (Mark 1:40-45) ......................................... 34

5. The Paralyzed Man: "Your sins are forgiven."
   (Mark 2:1-12) .......................................... 39

6. The Man with a Withered Hand:
   "He was grieved at their hardness of heart."
   (Mark 3:1-6) ........................................... 43

7. Calming the Storm: "Have you still no faith?"
   (Mark 4:35-41) ......................................... 48

8. The Gerasene Demoniac: "My name is Legion."
   (Mark 5:1-20) .......................................... 53

9. The Woman with a Hemorrhage:
   "Daughter, your faith has made you well."
   (Mark 5:21-42) ......................................... 58

10. The Gentile Woman's Daughter: "Even the dogs under the table eat the children's crumbs." (Mark 7:24-30) ........................................ 63

11. The Blind Man at Bethsaida: "I can see people, but they look like trees, walking." (Mark 8:22-26) ........................................ 67

12. The Spirit-Possessed Boy: "I believe; help my unbelief!" (Mark 9:14-29) ........................................ 71

13. The Withering of the Fig Tree: "Have faith in God." (Mark 11:12-14, 20-25) ........................................ 76

14. The Large Catch of Fish: "Go away from me, Lord, for I am a sinful man!" (Luke 5:1-11) ........................................ 81

15. Resuscitating a Widow's Son: "Do not weep." (Luke 7:11-17) ........................................ 86

16. The Bent-over Woman: "You are set free from your ailment." (Luke 13:10-17) ........................................ 91

17. The Man with Dropsy: "All who exalt themselves will be humbled." (Luke 14:1-24) ........................................ 97

18. The Samaritan Leper: "Were not ten made clean?" (Luke 17:11-19) ........................................ 103

19. A Blind-Mute Demoniac: "The kingdom of God has come to you." (Matthew 12:22-28) ........................................ 107

20. A Coin Found in a Fish: "The children are free." (Matthew 17:24-27) ........................................ 112

21. Changing Water into Wine: "What concern
    is that to you and to me?"
    (John 2:1-11) ............................................................. 118

22. The Royal Official's Son: "Sir, come down
    before my little boy dies."
    (John 4:46-54) ........................................................... 123

23. Healing the Paralyzed Man: "Do you want
    to be made well?"
    (John 5:1-18) ............................................................. 128

24. Feeding the Many: "Sir, give us this
    bread always."
    (John 6:1-14, 25-35) ................................................. 133

25. Walking on Water: "It is I; do not be afraid."
    (John 6:15-21) ........................................................... 138

26. Healing the Blind Man: "Do you also want to
    become his disciples?"
    (John 9:1-41) ............................................................. 143

27. The Raising of Lazarus: "Lord, he whom you
    love is ill."
    (John 11:1-46) ........................................................... 148

Notes ............................................................................ 153

Index of Scripture References ..................................... 154

Appendix: Synopsis Chart of Jesus' Miracles .......... 159

# Acknowledgments

As with most books, the name on the cover of this book does not accurately reflect all the people who were involved in its production. It is customary to acknowledge those who have been instrumental in the publication process; with gratitude I do so here. First, I would like to thank John McLaughlin for encouraging me to write this book and for contributing the Introduction. Thanks also to Kevin Burns at Novalis, who has been a supportive editor, and to Nancy Keyes, Jennifer Rae-Brown and Anne Louise Mahoney for their careful reading of the text. I owe a debt of gratitude to my research assistants at Queen's Theological College, who have helped in various capacities over the past two years. Nancy Wilson did background research for the book, while Erin Vearncombe and Helena Medeiros took particular care in editing the final draft. My spouse, Mary-Lynne Ascough, was a constant source of encouragement and practical advice, particularly in editing various drafts. My children, Hannah and Josiah, as always, provided a fulfilling diversion from my writing. Finally, my parents and my parents-in-law have been supportive of my writing and research endeavours, and so it is to them that I dedicate this book.

*Richard S. Ascough*

# Introduction

"And he cured many who were sick with various diseases, and cast out many demons..." (Mark 1:34). This summary statement, which comes early in Mark's Gospel, indicates that healing was a major element in Jesus' ministry. Just before this point in Mark's Gospel, Jesus has cast out an unclean spirit in the synagogue at Capernaum and healed Simon Peter's mother-in-law. In the chapters that follow, Jesus will perform more exorcisms and healings as well as "nature" miracles, such as calming a storm at sea. He will multiply bread and fish to feed thousands and will even raise people from the dead. Much of the other three Gospels also deal with Jesus' miracles. It is clear that the Gospel writers understood Jesus to be a miracle worker.

Most of us today do not experience Jesus in such terms, however. Such miracles are not part of our everyday lives. So how should we understand Jesus' miracles in the Gospels? Is the miraculous something restricted to the ancient past? Are the miracles nothing more than stories meant to highlight the importance of Jesus? In other words, are the miracles in the Gospels relevant for modern Christians?

If we consider the Gospels to be God's word, then our answer should be an emphatic *yes*! But the question still remains: *How* are these ancient miracles relevant for us today? The best way to approach this question is to look first at their relevance for the evangelists themselves and for their own audiences. Although they were much closer in time to Jesus than we are, each of the four Gospel writers still wrote well after the time of Jesus himself: the earliest, Mark, dates to about 40 years afterwards, while John, the latest, wrote about 65 years after Jesus' death and resurrection. The evangelists' purpose in writing was not just to tell Jesus' story, but also to reflect on the significance of Jesus' life, death and resurrection for their individual communities. Each was trying to answer the question "What does Jesus' ministry mean for us today?"

This series of books seeks to answer the same question for our contemporary world. Following the pattern of my book, *The Questions of Jesus* (Novalis, 2001), in this volume Richard Ascough focuses on Jesus' miracles. (Two other volumes will deal with Jesus' parables and teachings.) In order to demonstrate the relevance of Jesus' miracles for us today, Ascough first considers them in their own context: both the context of the Gospels themselves and the context of the first-century CE Mediterranean world.

Ascough illuminates the historical context of Jesus' miracles by examining them against the background of the First Testament as well as the social, political and economic reality of the Roman Empire. On the one hand, Jesus and his audience were thoroughly familiar with the First Testament, which tells of God's involvement with the Jewish people. In the Scriptures, God regularly intervened in the history of the people, setting them free from slavery in Egypt, establishing them in Israel, correcting them when they strayed and accepting them back when they repented. Frequently during their history the Jews experienced God working miracles on their behalf, whether it was their escape from the Egyptians through the Red Sea (Exodus 14–15) or the preservation of Jerusalem from the superior forces of the Assyrian army (Isaiah 36–37). Jesus and his contemporaries knew God as one who was involved in human affairs. At the same time, Jesus and his countrymen and -women were not free. They, God's chosen people, were under the rule of the Romans, who controlled the entire Mediterranean world, including Galilee and Judea, where Jesus performed his miracles. Both those factors – the belief that God wanted them to be free and the fact that they were not – form the background to the Gospel miracles.

At the same time, within the Gospels themselves the miracles play an important part in communicating the authors' message. Mark summarizes Jesus' preaching in these words: "The time is fulfilled, and the kingdom of God has come near" (Mark 1:15). He did not mean just another political system replacing the Roman Empire, but specifically one in which God's will was put into effect. When we read the traditional phrase "the kingdom of God" we should think of God's active "kingship" or "reign" in the world. In other words, a reference to God's "kingdom" indicates that God is in control, that God's plan for us is put into effect. Part of God's plan is that we be free from sickness and death, and especially that we be free from the control of Satan. Through his healings and exorcisms Jesus establishes the kingdom he preaches. His miracles show that God's reign has, in fact, begun. By casting out demons Jesus breaks the power of Satan and brings about God's reign in place of the devil's control, but for the ancient world, sickness and death were also linked to Satan. The Wisdom of Solomon tells us that death came into the world through the envy of the devil (2:24), and since sickness and disease often lead to death, they too represented the influence of the devil (compare Romans 5:12). Jesus' healing miracles demonstrate that God's rule has come into the world and has overcome the power of the devil as much as his exorcisms did.

Another element of Jesus' miracles is one we often miss. Because of the limited medical knowledge of the time, many diseases that today can easily be controlled or even cured were then highly contagious. As a result, the sick were often avoided. Add to this the perceived connection between sickness and the devil, and many viewed the sick as both physically and morally contaminated, to be shunned and excluded from everyday society. By healing the sick, Jesus brings them back into relationship with others, thereby further establishing the community that constitutes the kingdom of God.

In each chapter of this book, Ascough discusses a different miracle against the background of this understanding of Jesus' ministry in the ancient world. In doing so he provides insight into what the story would have meant for those who heard or read it for the first time. He then reflects on the episodes in terms of their relevance for us today, helping the miracles take on fuller meaning for the faith life of modern believers.

Some of the words and phrases used in this book may require an explanation. First, traditional terminology for the two main divisions of the Bible is problematic and has implications for how one interprets both of those sections. "Old Testament" connotes "antiquated," "outdated" and even "replaced" for some. "Hebrew Bible" is popular in many circles, but designating the material by its (primary) language of composition does not take into account those parts of Daniel and Ezra that were written in Aramaic or the extensive scholarly use of ancient versions in other languages, to say nothing of the second part of the Bible, which still tends to be called the "New Testament." "Hebrew Bible" also does not incorporate the deutero-canonical books, some written exclusively in Greek, which Roman Catholics and Eastern Orthodox Christians consider scriptural but Protestants and Jews do not. Similarly, "Jewish Bible/Scripture" is inadequate for Christians in general, for whom the first part of the Bible is also part of their Scriptures. As an uneasy compromise, the terms "First Testament" and "Second Testament" are used in this book for the two main divisions of the biblical literature.

Second, in the following pages the phrase "Synoptic Gospels" is used in reference to the Gospels of Matthew, Mark and Luke. These three are called "synoptic" because, in contrast to the Fourth Gospel (John), their presentation of Jesus can be seen (-optic) together (syn-). They can be arranged in three parallel columns, and different editions of such a synopsis have been published. Once they are viewed side by side in this way it becomes clear that Matthew, Mark and Luke describe the same basic events from the life of Jesus in roughly the same order and often with the exact same words. This suggests that there is a literary relationship among those three Gospels, such that two of the authors have copied significant portions from one or two of the others. The most commonly accepted solution to this "synoptic problem" is that Matthew and Luke, working independently of each other, followed the narrative outline and content of Mark, but also supplemented him with material taken from a collection of Jesus' sayings. This second source is designated with the letter "Q," from the German word *Quelle,* which simply means "source."

Ascough's treatment of the individual miracles is consistent with this solution. He starts with miracles found in Mark's Gospel, the first to be written, then follows these with miracles from Luke and Matthew. He ends with John's own distinctive miracles. But at times when he is discussing a miracle from Mark he will note how Matthew or Luke may have adapted it in order to reflect their own specific concerns.

Third, "the LORD" is used in place of the name of the God of Israel. Even though the name is present in the ancient Hebrew manuscripts of the First Testament, a growing sense of the sacredness of both God and God's name, plus a concern that one might even inadvertently take God's name in vain, eventually led to the practice of not pronouncing the name that was written. Instead, to this day observant Jews substitute the term *adonai* ('ădōnāy), which means "my Lord," wherever the name itself appears. In keeping with this practice, except for Chapter 25, where the name is central to the point being made, "the LORD" is used in place of the divine name, but it is written in capital letters to signify that God's name is meant and not just the word "lord."

Finally, the abbreviations BCE and CE are used. These stand for "Before the Common Era" and "Common Era." They cover the same period as BC ("Before Christ") and AD (*"Anno Domini"* = "The Year of the Lord"), but the first set of abbreviations is more commonly used by biblical scholars than is the latter.

Each of the following chapters begins with a reference indicating where the specific miracle to be discussed can be found in one of the Gospels. Reading *about* the Bible should not take the place of reading the Bible itself, so read each passage before reading the chapter. This book uses the New Revised Standard Version (NRSV) when quoting from the Bible, but any modern translation will do. Differences in wording among translations are usually the result of the different translators' choices as to how to render a word that has more than one nuance. Such matters should not be allowed to interfere with letting the biblical texts come alive for you today, which is the purpose of this book. To that end, open your heart to hear God speak through these reflections on God's own word.

*John L. McLaughlin*
*Toronto, Ontario*
*February 24, 2003*

# 1

# Jesus the Miracle Worker

"He cured many who were sick."
Mark 1:32-34

Although today we might differentiate between "demon-possession" and a physical illness, such was not the case in antiquity. If we say someone is sick today, we mean that they have some medical problem that a physician will attempt to remedy. Our medical knowledge, although not complete, is advanced and we know of agents such as cancer cells, bacteria and viruses that cause illnesses. We either know of, or are working on, medical treatments for curing illness. People who are sick in our society may need to be isolated either for their own sake (recovery) or the sake of others (transmission), but normally this is voluntary. While in the past persons who had severe physical or mental disabilities were marginalized, today attempts are made to integrate them into society.

In antiquity, illness was not understood in medical terms. One became sick not through viruses but through punishment by the gods (for sin), curses, ritual impurity or the activity of demons. Thus, Luke thinks nothing of reporting that an ill woman has been "bound" by Satan for 18 years (Luke 13:16). The more severe the illness, it was assumed, the more severe the transgression that provoked it. People with minor ailments were often ostracized. Those with more severe ailments ("handicaps") were treated as outcasts and could be forced to live outside the boundaries of villages and cities. They were barred from participation in community events. Such people stood little chance of succeeding (or surviving) in society. Few lived long once illness struck.

The role of the healer in ancient society was to restore people to their rightful place within the community. While we may be tempted to see Jesus as a healer whose primary ministry was the alleviation of physical suffering, his ability to heal social suffering was more important. Jesus, as a healer, not only cured physical ailments (as would a doctor), but in doing so restored people to their place in the community. It is in such a context that we will place Jesus' miracles in the chapters that follow.

In the "Synoptic Gospels" (so named because they can be "seen together"), Mark, Matthew and Luke present Jesus as a miracle worker. Jesus performed a total of 29 miracles before his passion and resurrection (in which, of course, the greatest miracle of all occurred). We will look at a number of these miracles in the next 19 chapters of the book. Overall, the miracles show that while Jesus *preached* the in-breaking of the kingdom of God, he *demonstrated* its arrival through mighty works or miracles. For the Gospel writers, preaching and demonstration go hand in hand. Miracles also demonstrate Jesus' concern for all people – there are no ethnic, social or gender barriers to God's care. Finally, and perhaps most importantly, Jesus' miracles demonstrate God's care for the whole person – Jesus' healings integrated persons back into society as a whole. In performing miracles, Jesus was carrying out his ministry "to proclaim release to the captives and recovery of sight to the blind, to let the oppressed go free" (Luke 4:18).

One might ask whether miracles happen today; certainly the Bible does not rule them out. However, extraordinary miracles seem to be rare. We risk setting up false hopes for the sick if we treat extraordinary miracles as regular and to be expected. While Jesus healed many, he did not heal everyone. Sickness, disease and death are still with us, at least while we await the full manifestation of God's kingdom on earth. However, whenever relationships are restored, faith is strengthened. When people recover from illness, we see signs of God's involvement in our lives. From the perspective of faith, God can be understood to be working in extraordinary ways in each of our lives. Such miracles are signs of God's restoration of order in a disorderly, broken world.

It is with this concern for the faith perspective that we will, in the final seven chapters of this book, turn our attention to the miracles in the fourth Gospel. Like the Synoptic Gospels, the

Gospel of John presents the story of Jesus' ministry, death and resurrection. Yet, when we compare the fourth Gospel to the other three Gospels, we quickly realize that the story told in John has a different overall theology. Although John includes episodes and sayings from Jesus' public ministry, much of his narrative is taken up with the intimate discourse between Jesus and his disciples. These distinctions reflect, in part, the fact that John is writing to a different community, in a different time and place, with different questions about Jesus' identity and ministry. One of the most significant differences between John's Gospel and the other three Gospels is the inclusion of only seven miracles, or "signs," as John prefers to call them. Of these, only two overlap with the 29 miracles recounted in the other three Gospels. The seven "signs" in John's Gospel were chosen with care and reflect John's particular concerns.

Included in John's Gospel are three nature miracles, in which Jesus shows his power over the natural elements, and four healing miracles, in which Jesus shows his power over illness and death. Some scholars suggest that these seven miracles originally formed a shorter Gospel, deemed the "signs Gospel" (from references in 2:11; 4:54; 6:14; 9:16; 11:45; cf. 12:18), which had grown in importance to the people in John's church. In fact, the "signs Gospel" was probably used as an evangelizing tool to give demonstrations ("signs") that Jesus was the Messiah. For this reason, John also included the miracles in the larger work that he was writing, which suggests that they now presuppose a faith perspective. While on the one hand the miracles are written to inspire belief in Jesus, on the other hand they are meant to speak deeply to those who already believe in Jesus. We will focus our study on these two aspects of the importance of miracles in John's Gospel.

# 2

# The Synagogue Demoniac

"I know who you are."
Mark 1:21-28

The exorcism of a demon in a synagogue is the first of a number of exorcisms that Jesus performs in the Synoptic Gospels. In Mark's Gospel it comes shortly after Jesus' baptism and temptation and follows immediately upon his calling of the first disciples. This inaugural event in Jesus' ministry defines the primary way that Jesus will interact with others. There are other ways, such as conversations, preaching and debates, but, according to the Gospel writers, it is Jesus' role as a miracle worker that first attracted large crowds and put him in line with the group of ancient wonder-workers also known as "magicians."

There are numerous stories in antiquity, in both Jewish and "pagan" literature, of magicians who work wonders. For example, the late first-century CE Jewish historian Josephus tells the story of a man named Eleazar who, in the presence of the emperor Vespasian, uses special incantations and a ring with roots prescribed by Solomon in it to cure a demon-possessed man. To prove that the exorcism was effective, and to impress his audience, Eleazar sets up a pitcher of water and commands the demon to knock it over on its way out.'[1] What is striking about such stories is that behind each one, a particular literary pattern can be determined: a description of the demon-possessed person; opposition to the healer; a command against the demon, often accompanied by a physical action; a demonstration of success; the reaction of the observers. We see this pattern, with only slight variation, in the stories of Jesus' exorcisms and healings, including the exorcism of Mark 1:21-28.

The exorcism story opens with a description of the problem: "a man with an unclean spirit" (v. 23). The demons within the man cause him to call out to Jesus, "What have you to do with us, Jesus of Nazareth? Have you come to destroy us?" (v. 24). The demons do not cry out in fear but in derision, their voices dripping with sarcasm, for it seems they have the edge in the encounter. Their edge is their knowledge of Jesus' true identity: "I know who you are," one spirit says, "the Holy One of God" (v. 24).

In antiquity, miracle workers such as Jesus were known to have secret identities revealed to them by their divine patron in a vision. Likewise, demons had a secret identity, one given to them by their overlord, the prince of demons. This secret identity was not to be revealed to anyone, for if it was, the one to whom it was revealed could gain mastery over the other. Such mastery was referred to as "name-magic."

For the ancient reader of this story, the end is assured. The demons will conquer Jesus, leaving him dead or worse, for they have ascertained his secret identity. The demons have access to a powerful god who has given them this knowledge. Humans are unlikely to gain access to such a high level. Thus, at the very least, the audience would expect a difficult and perhaps bloody battle to ensue. But the demons' name-magic has no effect on Jesus, who responds, "Be silent, and come out of him!" (v. 25). At this command, the demons leave the man, giving a loud wail to show the effectiveness of the exorcism.

Our familiarity with this story and other stories like it reduces its effect on us. In light of Jesus' overall ministry, and especially his resurrection, we know that he will win this encounter. Yet, for the first-time audience, and even within the first generation of Christians, this early miracle of Jesus must have stood out. Here is a miracle worker who is different! Rather than being defeated by name-magic, or even relying on it, he gives a command and the exorcism occurs. Just how unusual this was is conveyed in the final aspect of the story, where the crowd reacts with amazement, asking, "What is this? A new teaching – with authority! He commands even the unclean spirits, and they obey him" (v. 27). They want to know who it is that can exorcise a demon with a command, even in a situation in which his true identity is known. Because the demons know Jesus' name, they should have won, but Jesus is more powerful than they are.

For Mark's original readers, and for us, the surprise of Jesus' victory is somewhat mitigated because we, too, know who Jesus is. Mark begins his narrative with the words "The beginning of the good news of Jesus Christ, the Son of God" (Mark 1:1). So while it takes some time for the disciples to realize the full implications of Jesus' identity – it is not until Chapter 8 that Peter makes his confession, saying, "You are the Messiah" (Mark 8:29) – the reader knows it already. Thus, the first miracle serves to confirm this identity and to build confidence that the "Son of God" designation is not to be taken lightly. Jesus has real power that is directly related to the most-high God.

This miracle, however, challenges us today. How do we appropriate such a story into our own world view, one in which the physical location of God's throne up and slightly to the left of the stars is not operative? One possible response is to dismiss the story as mythic nonsense. At the other extreme, we could become demon-hunters, finding possessed victims at every turn and drawing upon the power of Jesus to exorcise them. But for the everyday Christian neither extreme seems likely, or even possible. Our faith calls us to take these stories seriously, yet our world view causes us to apply them differently.

At the core of our story is a message of confidence in Jesus' power in people's lives. Although Jesus chose a path of suffering and weakness, it was a deliberate choice. His power over demonic forces suggests that he could easily have escaped his death sentence. Yet his choosing to suffer continues to bring hope and healing to millions of people. Whereas some might see defeat in Jesus' death, we find victory in his resurrection. Just as name-magic does not triumph over Jesus, so death does not defeat him. Death has not disappeared from our world. But Jesus will triumph over it for all who are his disciples.

# 3

# Simon Peter's Mother-in-Law

"She began to serve them."
Mark 1:29-31

In urban and rural Palestine, and under Roman law generally, the oldest male was the head of the household, the *paterfamilias*. All other members of the household were under his authority, including children, grandchildren, slaves and even employees, if the *paterfamilias* happened to be a landowner or manufacturer. This is what is meant by a "patriarchal society": it is a social and cultural system in which a few men have power over others, particularly women, children and slaves, although often other men as well. Since the Second Testament is written in this context, we should not be surprised that it reflects the predominant socio-cultural system of its writers and readers.

Simon Peter's mother-in-law lives in Peter's house, which suggests that she was a widow and likely had no son or brother who would fulfill the role of guardian. In such cases it fell, by custom if not by law, upon one of the sons-in-law to take his wife's mother into his house. As a full member of the household and as a female, she was expected to fulfill certain domestic duties, particularly around food and hospitality. However, her ability to perform these duties is at risk since she lies ill with fever. Although not without compassion, the ancients still feared those who were ill because of the connection between illness and God's punishment. Thus, while she is now under Peter's roof, she may eventually have to be removed for fear that the entire household will be contaminated.

The story itself follows the typical pattern of a healing story. After leaving the synagogue and entering Simon's house, Jesus is told of the woman's ailment. Implied is an invitation to Jesus to do something about it. The miracle itself is almost nondescript, a contrast to the riotous synagogue exorcism narrated only a few verses earlier. Jesus takes the woman by the hand and lifts her up. As a result the fever leaves her and, Mark tells us, "she began to serve them" (Mark 1:31).

This final aspect of the healing of Peter's mother-in-law – "she began to serve them" – has always made this one of the more troubling miracles for me. I picture an elderly woman, frail and dehydrated from her fever, being compelled to get Jesus and his friends some refreshing wine and hors d'oeuvres. Of course, my picture is nonsense! That she gets up to serve them is not simply the reaffirmation of traditional female roles. Rather, her action shows that she has been restored to her function within the household. She has not only physically recovered; she has been healed socially, so that she no longer faces expulsion from the extended family due to her inability to contribute to it.

It is instructive to look at some slight differences in Luke's telling of this same miracle (Luke 4:38-39). Luke describes the fever as "high," thus showing the urgency of the need for healing. He also notes the immediacy of the mother-in-law's response to Jesus' actions. The most significant difference, however, is in Jesus' action itself. In Mark, Jesus takes Peter's mother-in-law by the hand; this gesture brings about the healing. In Luke, the touch is dropped to emphasize a healing word – Luke tells us that Jesus speaks and the fever leaves. While it is fully possible that Jesus both takes her hand (Mark) and speaks (Luke), for our purposes what is significant is where each author places the emphasis.

Elsewhere in his Gospel, Luke notes that Jesus heals through the laying on of hands (Luke 4:40). By emphasizing that Jesus heals through words in this case, Luke must want to draw our attention to a particular feature of this healing. Note the word that Luke uses to describe Jesus' manner of speaking: Jesus "rebuked" the fever. This is the same word that both Luke and Mark use to describe how Jesus speaks to the demon in the healing of the demon-possessed man in the synagogue – "Jesus rebuked him" (Luke 4:35; Mark 1:25). By "rebuking" the fever, Luke treats it as if it were produced by a demon which, in antiquity, would be the prevailing notion. Thus, as with an exorcism, this healing demonstrates Jesus' power over forces stronger than humans.

The account of the healing of Peter's mother-in-law is striking in its brevity. It is told without elaboration or comment. Despite the prominence of Peter among the 12 primary followers of Jesus, nowhere does Jesus ever remind Peter of this deed, nor does Peter refer to it. And yet, it must stand out for Peter among all of Jesus' miracles, since it has touched him personally in his home life. Indeed, it may have provided the impetus for Peter to follow Jesus beyond the immediate vicinity of his home city. Earlier in Mark's narrative, Jesus meets Simon along the Sea of Galilee and invites him and his brother Andrew, along with James and John, to follow him (Mark 1:16-20). Leaving their nets they seem to walk with him for less than a week before they come on the Sabbath to Peter's hometown of Capernaum. It is on this day that Jesus heals Peter's mother-in-law, immediately after synagogue.

The next day Jesus goes out early to a "deserted place" (Mark 1:35) and "Simon and his companions hunted for him" (1:36). Peter, the first of those called to follow Jesus, now becomes a leader among them, guiding them in their search for Jesus. When they find Jesus, he announces that their travels will be expanded beyond Capernaum into the whole region of Galilee. Peter's developing leadership and his willingness to follow Jesus pivot on the healing of his mother-in-law. Ironically, while his mother-in-law is restored to her role in the household, Peter breaks out of his role to follow Jesus.

Jesus' call to discipleship is not a command. It is an invitation. Peter is invited to follow, but before the full commitment is made, Jesus becomes personally involved in Peter's life by healing his mother-in-law. The same is true for us. Following Jesus is not an abstract response to a divine command. Rather, when we answer Jesus' call to follow him we invite him to change our personal lives. This might not always be as dramatic or as concrete as the healing of Peter's mother-in-law. The results, however, might cause us to shift radically our own priorities, as Peter did.

# 4

# A Man with Leprosy

"If you choose, you can make me clean."
Mark 1:40-45

In antiquity, any sort of unexplained rash or abnormal skin discolouration would be considered "leprous," since the designation "leprosy" referred to all sorts of skin diseases, not just the condition we now call Hansen's disease. According to Leviticus 13:45-46, lepers were to be distinctly identifiable at all times:

> The person who has the leprous disease shall wear torn clothes and let the hair of his head be disheveled; and he shall cover his upper lip and cry out, "Unclean, unclean." He shall remain unclean as long as he has the disease; he is unclean. He shall live alone; his dwelling shall be outside the camp.

In this way, the lepers' status as social outcasts would be obvious, even if their leprosy was not. They were to live alone outside the city, although they were allowed to beg at the city gate or village entrance during the day.

In a culture where family and social connections were strong, being put out of the community for any period of time was devastating. Unlike our own culture, where individualism and self-sufficiency are held in high regard, in antiquity one relied on others to meet basic needs. Thus, by being put out of the community, one's life could be at risk, even if the disease itself posed no problem. To combat the isolation and risks of living alone outside the community, "lepers" often banded together to form their own type of community. In doing so, the fear of contamination and ritual pollution was lessened by the knowledge that all were already outcasts from the wider society.

In the miracle story in Mark 1:40-45, we see a threefold pattern occurring twice: request, response, result. In the first cycle, the request comes from the leper, who comes begging and kneels before Jesus with his confident proclamation: "If you choose, you can make me clean" (1:40). It is striking that Jesus never heals anyone without their consent, or the consent of their friends and family. In response to this first request Jesus, who is moved with pity, reaches out and touches the man. However, rather than saying, "Be healed," Jesus says, "Be made clean," which is, quite literally, "Be washed" (1:41). Such wording recalls the healing of the Syrian general Naaman's leprosy in 2 Kings 5. In that story, the prophet Elisha tells Naaman to wash himself in the Jordan River seven times. When he does so, Naaman's skin "was restored like the flesh of a young boy, and he was clean" (2 Kings 5:14).

The result of Jesus' touch is immediate: "The leprosy left him, and he was made clean" (Mark 1:42). In contrast to the story of Naaman, where the healing required an extended action of washing, Jesus is able to produce a much quicker solution to the problem. The repetition of the word "clean" (literally, "washed") suggests that this aspect of the story is not accidental. The focus of this healing is on the social healing as much as the physical one. No longer is the man physically marred, and no longer can he be considered an outcast from the city. By touching the leper, Jesus not only heals him, he shows a willingness to flout societal opinion and Jewish law. Jesus considers the man to be fully human even in his unclean state.

At this point the story shifts to the second cycle of request, response, result. This time, things do not go quite so well. Jesus makes a request of the now-clean leper, telling him not to speak to anyone but to show himself to the priest and to offer up the appropriate sacrifices (1:43). The priest would carefully inspect the man's body to ensure that no traces of the skin disease remain. Once that had been ascertained, the priest would prescribe the sacrifices to be made, and the religious authorities would officially declare the man to be clean. He would then be able to re-enter the city for good. The public sacrifice that he would make would signal to the others living in that place that he had been certified as clean.

The man's response to Jesus' directive is to do the opposite. Rather than saying nothing to anyone, the man "went out and began to proclaim it freely, and to spread the word" (1:45). As a result, Jesus could no longer openly enter cities and villages but had to remain outside them. Although this did not limit his popularity – people came to him from every quarter – it did restrict his movement. Thus, we see in this miracle a reversal of fortunes. The once-marginalized man can now walk the city streets as a whole person, while the once-free healer is now forced to dwell on the margins since he can no longer walk freely in the cities and villages.

There is a message for us in this story concerning the place of the marginalized and outcasts of society. In proclaiming and manifesting the kingdom of God on earth, Jesus willingly brings healing and social reintegration to those who need it most. While we might not be able to perform physical healings, as Jesus' followers we are called to reach out and touch those whom others have abandoned. Although the First Testament contains stories about God giving leprosy as a punishment for sin (see Numbers 12:9-12; 2 Kings 5:27, 15:5; 2 Chronicles 26:19-23), note that Jesus makes no comment on the man's spiritual life. Rather, he focuses on the man's social condition, cleansing him in such a way that the man can function fully within society.

This story holds a warning for us. We have a tendency to strike bargains with God. We ask God to do something for us – such as provide a job, bring healing, ensure safety – and promise that if God delivers we will perform a particular deed, perhaps a good work or regular church attendance. Yet, as this story shows, we easily ignore even simple requests that God makes of us. In our excitement when God has met our needs, we rush about proclaiming our joy and sharing our good fortune. Yet God awaits our proper response. We must ask ourselves: Does our response to God show how we follow God, or does it drive God away?

# 5

# The Paralyzed Man

"Your sins are forgiven."
Mark 2:1-12

This miracle story contrasts faithful friends with unfaithful foes. The opening of the story illustrates the commitment of a paralyzed man's friends in bringing him to Jesus. When Jesus observes their faith in action (note that it is not the faith of the paralytic that is highlighted), he announces that the man's sins are forgiven. This statement provokes a reaction from the scribes, whose own lack of faith causes them to question Jesus' authority to make such a pronouncement.

We noted in Chapter 1 of this book that in antiquity, illness was seen as an indication of divine displeasure, notably a punishment for a particular sin committed by the person affected. In such cases, people who were ill were often cast out of the village and left without the support of friends or family. In this story we find an exception to this practice. The friends of a paralyzed man have committed themselves to caring for him. They are willing to carry him through the town in order to bring him to where Jesus is speaking.

Unlike other miracle stories where Jesus is approached and asked to come and heal someone, in this instance the sick person is brought to Jesus.

After arriving at the house only to find the crowds spilling out into the street, the friends push their faith one step further: "They removed the roof above him" (Mark 2:4). This brief statement does not do justice to the work that must have been involved in getting the paralyzed man onto the roof. The houses in Galilean villages such as Capernaum were generally single-storey buildings with a flat roof made of sticks and packed earth. Although there were often stone steps up to the roof, carrying a man on a pallet would have been difficult. Doing so without being noticed would be even trickier!

Jesus' response to the "raising of the roof" is surprising. This is the fourth miracle recorded in Mark's Gospel. The other three have followed the usual pattern of description, invitation and healing. Thus, we might expect that upon seeing the faith of the paralytic's friends, Jesus would reach out and touch the man, restoring the use of his legs. Rather, Mark breaks the pattern and describes the controversy that ensues when Jesus claims, "Son, your sins are forgiven" (2:5). This controversy is bracketed by the narrator's words "he said to the paralytic," which occur in verse 5b and again in verse 10b. When Mark brings us back to the paralytic, Jesus does indeed heal the man, commanding him to stand up, pick up his mat and go home. Although one might think the man would linger to thank Jesus, or perhaps hear more of his teachings, he does not. Without a word, he does as Jesus commands.

The paralyzed man is not much of a character in this story. He is the focal point of the action, but in contrast to his friends and the scribes, his character is undeveloped. This suggests that the message of this story lies not in the healing itself but in the actions of the faithful friends and the unfaithful foes. We noted above the friends' commitment to seeing the paralyzed man healed. But what do we make of the response of Jesus' foes?

Having forgiven the paralytic, Jesus perceives that the scribes are struggling with questions. "Why does this fellow speak in this way?" they ask. "Who can forgive sins but God alone?" They draw the obvious conclusion: "It is blasphemy!" (2:7). Hearing their muttering, he challenges the scribes, asking them which is easier to say: "Your sins are forgiven" or "Stand up and walk." It is a strange question to ask.

From the scribes' point of view, "Your sins are forgiven" is indeed harder to say. In saying "Stand up and walk," Jesus runs the risk only of being ridiculed when nothing happens (remember, we are viewing things from the scribes' perspective). However, in saying "Your sins are forgiven," Jesus runs the risk of being stoned to death for blasphemy since, as the scribes rightly point out, only God can make such a statement. Jesus' response to the faith of the friends of the paralyzed man is to say the more difficult of the two statements.

Without giving the scribes a chance to answer his question, Jesus utters the second statement, commanding the paralytic to stand up, pick up his mat and return home. The man immediately does what Jesus commands, lending credence to Jesus' earlier claim to forgive sins. Although the physical healing impresses the crowd, the forgiveness of sins should have impressed them more. Their claim "We have never seen anything like this!" (v. 12) flies in the face of the earlier story of the healing of the demoniac in the Capernaum synagogue. Since Capernaum was a small fishing village, it is likely that they had seen something similar, or had at least heard of it. What has not happened before is Jesus' bold claim to forgive sins. This claim anticipates his death, which will preclude the need for the forgiveness of sins to be mediated through animal sacrifices at the temple.

This miracle challenges us, for we are not able to replicate it. We cannot, for example, seek out Jesus by tearing the roof from a church in order to lower our friends for healing! Thus, we need to look for other ways to allow it to touch our lives. Certainly one of the most telling aspects of this miracle is the faithfulness of the paralytic's friends. Their efforts in bringing this man to Jesus are rewarded by Jesus' words to him: "Your sins are forgiven." We, too, can bring individuals before God in prayer. Whether they are in need of physical or spiritual healing, our committed and sustained prayer shows our belief that God can break into the natural order of this world and act on others' behalf.

# 6

# The Man with a Withered Hand

"He was grieved at their hardness of heart."
Mark 3:1-6

Compassion is an elusive commodity these days. In a world filled with suffering, war and terror, we can easily become desensitized to the plight of others. In faraway countries and in our neighbourhoods there are people in need of a compassionate word or gesture. Increasingly, however, North American culture is moving towards an emphasis on justice. In itself, justice is not a bad thing. However, justice must be balanced by compassion. When one or the other element is missing, life becomes unbalanced.

In the miraculous cure of the man with the withered hand, we see the tension between compassion and justice being played out. Jesus has already healed on the Sabbath, which went against Jewish law; this set the Pharisees against him. However, the miracle we are examining here represents the first time that Jesus' healing on the Sabbath sparks a reaction in the Pharisees. The story follows directly upon the controversy with the Pharisees over grain picked by Jesus and his disciples on the Sabbath. Jesus concludes that encounter with the words "The sabbath was made for humankind, and not humankind for the sabbath; so the Son of Man is lord even of the sabbath" (Mark 2:27-28). As if to reinforce his point, Jesus goes into the synagogue, probably the one at Capernaum, and does something that goes against the Pharisees' prevailing understanding of Torah (the law).

In *The Questions of Jesus,* the first volume in this series, John McLaughlin points out that the Pharisees had a good reason for insisting that no work be done on the Sabbath in order to keep it holy.[2] Exodus 20:8-11 states that the seventh day of the week is to be set apart as a day of rest in imitation of God resting on the final day of creation. Despite their reputation to the contrary, the Pharisees did not strive to be hypocritical. Having first established themselves as a group of *hasidim*, "pious ones," in support of the second-century BCE Jewish rebellion against the encroachment of Greek culture, they came to be known as the "separated ones," or "Pharisees." They were not priests but lay teachers and experts in the law. Their relationship with God was not centred on the temple ritual but on obedience to all 613 laws in the Pentateuch. For them, the law of Moses was a living code that needed constant interpretation, thus they built on and preserved the traditions and teachings of the great scribes and teachers. These interpretations were then taught in the synagogues that they established throughout the land.

The Pharisees' were greatly concerned with obedience to Torah as an expression of their faith in God and as a response to God's grace towards them. At some point, however, they lost sight of human compassion. Their insistence that no work be done on the Sabbath ignored another essential aspect of the Sabbath – its distinction from the regular routine of the other six days of the week (Deuteronomy 5:12-15). This is what truly demarcates the Sabbath.

Jesus does not advocate a wholesale abandonment of Sabbath observance. He claims, "Do not think that I have come to abolish the law or the prophets; I have come not to abolish but to fulfill" (Matthew 5:17). Thus, his healing on the Sabbath should not be understood as a revolutionary action seeking to overturn Torah. Instead, Jesus uses the opportunity to remind the Pharisees that Torah's concern for justice and right action is mediated with its equally important concern for compassion and love. Jesus poses this question: "Is it lawful to do good or to do harm on the sabbath, to save life or to kill?" (Mark 3:4). This is not an either/or proposition about a particular course of action. Jesus is not asking, "Should I help this man, or should I hurt him further?" Jesus is posing two separate questions: "Is it lawful to do good on the Sabbath?" and "Is it lawful to do harm on the Sabbath?"

The Pharisees' silence angers Jesus because the answers to his questions are obvious. One of the ten primary commandments of Torah is "You shall not murder" (Exodus 20:13). Leviticus 24:17 states that "Anyone who kills a human being shall be put to death," an injunction that is repeated for emphasis only four verses later (24:21). While on the surface it seems contradictory to prescribe death for anyone who kills a person (would not the executioner then need to die?), the Leviticus texts point to a prohibition on killing another person outside of Torah: that is, taking justice into one's own hands (see Numbers 35:16-31). In contrast, Torah puts a heavy emphasis on mercy and love. The Pharisees were well aware of the summary of Torah in the words "You shall love the Lord your God with all your heart, and with all your soul, and with all your mind...and you shall love your neighbour as yourself." This composite of Deuteronomy 6:4 and Leviticus 19:18 was quoted by Jesus (Mark 12:29-31), Paul (Romans 13:9; Galatians 5:14), and James (James 2:8). This statement had been used to summarize Torah for some time before the first century. Underlying the saying is Torah's revelation that compassion is at the core of God's being – "I am compassionate" (Exodus 22:27). This underlying compassion should have been obvious to the Pharisees who opposed Jesus. Indeed, it probably was obvious, which may be why they remained silent rather than answering Jesus' questions.

Whatever the understanding of the Pharisees was, Jesus does not wait to engage them further in debate. Turning to the man with the withered hand, Jesus gives a command: "Stretch out your hand," he says, and the ailment is healed. The Pharisees' desire to triumph over Jesus immediately sends them out of the synagogue to seek out another group, the Herodians, to help them. We know little about this enigmatic group of Herodians. All we can gather from their name is that they were affiliated with the families of Herod the Great and thus aligned with the power brokers of the day. As such, they would have had little sympathy for the cause of a Galilean peasant such as Jesus.

This miracle presents contrasting views of our responsibility in serving God. On the one hand, there is the group of Pharisees who, despite their knowledge of Torah's emphasis on compassion, are more interested in regulating people's behaviour. On the other hand, there is Jesus, who sees a person's need overriding strict adherence to a code of conduct. As twenty-first-century Christians, we may find it easy to point the finger back through time and accuse the Pharisees of hypocritical behaviour. This can, however, blind us to our own reliance on justice and law over compassion. We are called to move beyond a judgmental attitude. For example, it is easy to blame people who live on the street for being in this situation, but we do not know their stories. God does not call us to judge them. God calls us to say to them, "Stretch out your hand," and to take that hand and help the person along the path to wholeness.

# 7

# Calming the Storm

"Have you still no faith?"
Mark 4:35-41

The miracle of the calming of the storm is one of only seven miracles in which Jesus manifests his power over the forces of nature. Of those seven nature miracles, four involve water: two include fish (coin in the mouth; large catch of fish) and two include boats (calming the storm; walking on water). All four water miracles take place on the Sea of Galilee (as does the post-resurrection story of the large catch of fish in John 21:1-11). The "Sea" of Galilee is actually a freshwater lake and not a large one at that. It is only 20 kilometres (12.5 miles) long and 11 kilometres (7 miles) wide, with a shoreline circumference of 40 kilometres (25 miles). In the first century, as is the case today, it was well-stocked with fish, and many people who lived on its shore earned their living through fishing.

The "calming of the storm" miracle reflects a problem that fishermen frequently encounter on the Sea of Galilee. The sea lies 180 metres (600 feet) below sea level at the end of the long, deep gorge known as the Jordan River valley. The wind rushes down the valley, gaining speed along the way. By the time the wind reaches the sea itself, it can be ferocious, with sudden gusts that cause the sea to go from calm to filled with whitecap waves in a matter of minutes. Such occurrences strike fear in the heart of even the most seasoned sailor.

It is no surprise, then, that the disciples of Jesus are afraid when a great windstorm arises, even though many of them are fishermen. The story itself follows the pattern typical of miracle stories. A description of the problem is given first: a great storm swamps the disciples' boat. They decide to wake Jesus. In Mark's account their words seem to express no more than frustration with him – they seem to want him to be awake for their demise at sea. Matthew makes clear what is implicit in Mark's account – Jesus is being awoken to do something about the situation. The disciples cry out, "Lord, save us!" (Matthew 8:25). Yet in all three Synoptic Gospel accounts their reaction to the miracle clearly shows that they are not expecting Jesus to be able to take control of the storm the way he does: "Who then is this," they ask, "that even the wind and the sea obey him?" (Mark 4:41).

Jesus' response is to "rebuke" the wind and command the water to be at "peace." We noted in Chapter 2 of this book the significance of the word "rebuke" in Jesus' miracles. This word of command assumes that there is a divine being responsible for the natural forces that threaten his disciples' safety. It reveals the underlying understanding of people in antiquity that divine agents control all events, natural or otherwise, including weather, earthquakes, disease and fertility. The ensuing calm that follows Jesus' commands not only indicates his power over nature, but suggests to the observers that he has friends in high places. Indeed, the disciples' question, "Who then is this...?" is not a question about Jesus' identity but about where he figures in the hierarchy of powers.

One question that biblical interpreters often ask themselves is why a particular story about Jesus might have been preserved. If we take it as given that Jesus performed more miracles than those recorded in the four Gospels (cf. John 21:25), why were these ones written down? What did they say to the early Christians that was significant? In the case of the calming of the storm, some scholars suggest that the story itself, while it does show Jesus' place in the hierarchy of cosmic powers, is a metaphor for the faith of believers. The plight of those in the Church today is similar to the plight of those in the boat. Even when it is stormy Jesus is with us, yet for some reason we still panic!

Matthew's account of the miracle highlights this aspect of the story (Matthew 8:18, 23-27). After noting Jesus' intention to cross the sea, Matthew deliberately places within the narrative framework two sayings on discipleship that call for a radical break with the safety of home. In one, Jesus tells a would-be follower that, unlike foxes and birds, he has no permanent dwelling. In the other, Jesus tells another potential follower that the usual familial obligations, such as burial of family members, are to be abandoned. When the great storm hits the boat the cry for help in Matthew is a prayer: "Lord, save us! We are perishing!" (v. 25). The use of "Lord" reflects a confession of discipleship. In Matthew's Gospel, when Jesus awakes, he puts the disciples to shame for their "little faith" (v. 26), and then calms the seas.

The story as narrated by Matthew shows his audience, and us, the confidence we are to have in Jesus despite the storms we face as his disciples. In times of trouble we cry out in desperation for God to save us. While there is a place in the Christian tradition for petitionary prayer, this story suggests that it must arise out of a deep-seated faith in God rather than fear.

There is a story of a man who drew too close to the edge of a deep canyon, lost his footing, and plunged over the side. In desperation, on the way down he managed to grab onto a small bush on the side of the canyon wall. Filled with terror, he called out, "Is there anyone up there? Can anyone help me?"

A voice reassured him, saying, "I am here, the Lord your God." Relieved, the man expressed his appreciation for the presence of the Lord.

"Before I help you," said God, "I want to know whether you believe in me."

The man answered, "Lord, I certainly believe in you. I go to church every Sunday, and sometimes even on Wednesdays. I read my Bible regularly and pray each day."

God replied, "But do you really believe in me?"

"I do, I do," cried the man. "I believe!"

God said, "Good. Now let go of the branch." When the man stammered his objections God repeated, "If you believe in me, let go of the branch."

The man hesitated for a moment and then yelled, "Is there anyone else up there?"

God does not promise a life free of "dangers, toils and snares," in the words of the hymn "Amazing Grace." But unlike those in the boat with Jesus, or the man in the canyon, as Jesus' disciples we must rest assured in our faith that God is with us and is taking care of us.

# The Gerasene Demoniac

"My name is Legion."
Mark 5:1-20

The healing of the Gerasene demoniac is one of the strangest of all of the exorcisms Jesus performs, both in content and in the differences among the three Synoptic accounts. Mark opens the story by noting that the disciples and Jesus "came to the other side of the sea, to the country of the Gerasenes" (Mark 5:1), to which Luke adds the clarifying note that it was opposite Galilee (Luke 8:26). The country of the Gerasenes was 48 kilometres (30 miles) southeast of the Sea of Galilee, near the city of Gerasa. This distance is problematic, as the swine are said to have run into the sea. Recognizing that 48 kilometres is quite a distance for a herd of pigs to run, Matthew changes the location to the "country of the Gadarenes" (Matthew 8:28), which is much closer to the Sea of Galilee. However, it is still 9.5 kilometres (6 miles) southeast of the sea. In the later tradition, both places became conflated and identified with the similar sounding name Gergasa (modern Kursi), which was a city right on the lake, with tombs and a cliff in the vicinity.

All of this might seem like academic nit-picking were it not that this is only the beginning of what turns out to be a somewhat surreal miracle of Jesus. Since all of the above-named cities were Gentile, it does not matter which one is the actual location of the miracle. That the people of the city were Gentile is clear enough from the presence of a herd of swine. What is of greater interest is how this miracle changed through oral transmission. Mark likely wrote down the miracle in the late 60s of the first century, some 30 years after it happened. Before then it must have circulated orally among Christian groups, as Christians told one another stories about Jesus' mighty deeds. We should be able to discern what it was about this story that resonated with their faith.

As the story opens, we note that the man possessed (or, in Matthew's telling, the two possessed men) has been ostracized and is living among the tombs. Although very much alive, he is considered dangerous, and is forced to live as if he were dead. Mark paints a rather bleak picture of his existence, noting that he was wild beyond restraint, often abusing himself. Jesus commands the unclean spirit to depart from the man, but it refuses to obey. Instead, it causes the man to run towards Jesus, shouting, "What have you to do with me, Jesus, Son of the Most High God? I adjure you by God, do not torment me" (v. 7). As was the case with Jesus' first exorcism (the synagogue demoniac, Mark 1:23-26), this unclean spirit is privy to Jesus' "secret identity." By employing "name-magic" the spirit expects to be able to drive

Jesus away. The words do not reflect a plea but a command; they could perhaps be paraphrased as "in the name of God, go away." Together, the running, shouting and name-magic reflect the unclean spirit's attempt to repel Jesus.

In this particular instance – the only one in the Gospels – Jesus resorts to using name-magic. He gains power over the unclean spirit by learning its name. As it turns out, the unclean spirit is not one but many and goes by the name "Legion," a Roman military designation. In the early first century CE, a legion officially numbered 6,000 soldiers, although it was often smaller since there were not enough troops to staff all the existing legions. The connection between the designation "Legion" and the occupying force in the land of the Jews would be difficult to miss. The demons that live in the man behave like an occupying power; their one wish is to remain where they are not natives. The driving of the demon-possessed swine into the sea reflects the desire of the Jewish people to see the Romans driven out of their land. Thus, this story represents the transference of aggression from the Romans to the demons. It is a common strategy for oppressed groups, whose only hope of deliverance is through miraculous acts of God.

Although the connection between the demons and the Roman army was probably made in the early oral versions of this story, the Gospel stories do not highlight the connection. Luke makes it clear that demons had entered the man (Luke 8:30) and that Jesus has defeated Satan's "foot soldiers."

The language of "legion" is a military image used to describe Satan's army, not Rome's!

Either way, the point of the story is that Jesus has power over these malicious beings. No longer able to challenge Jesus, as they have lost the name-magic battle, they now resort to begging not to be exiled. With a twist of irony Jesus spares them exile by sending them into a herd of swine that is then propelled into the sea to drown. They have avoided exile, but the demons are now destroyed. When the people of the surrounding villages hear of the healing, they ask Jesus to depart from them. They are not really rejecting Jesus; they are afraid. In contrast to the awe that often greets Jesus' miracles in Galilee, this Gentile crowd expresses terror at the manifestations of supernatural powers.

This miracle reflects a complex narrative and an even more complex history. It is the task of biblical scholars to debate the details of the text. However, it is not without significance for us. At the very least, the way we have sorted out the story above shows us that the early Christians were not apolitical. In preserving a tradition that shows Jesus defeating a "legion" of demons, they give voice to a desire that the kingdom of God break into this world both spiritually and politically. Jesus' miracles show us that the incarnation carries with it profound implications for the in-breaking of the kingdom. We are called as followers of Jesus to participate in the political arena, working for a world in which those who oppress others will be cast into the sea. Such actions can trouble those who prefer to remain on the sidelines, as the Gerasene villagers did. However, opposition should not deter us from action. Like the healed man, we are to proclaim what Jesus does for us, spiritually *and* politically, throughout the land.

# 9

# The Woman with a Hemorrhage

"Daughter, your faith has made you well."
Mark 5:21-42

The story of the miracle of the woman with a long-lasting hemorrhage is found in the middle of the story of the raising of Jairus' daughter. Although each of these two miracles is important in its own right, they are more powerful when narrated together, as Mark underlines with his parenthetical statement at the conclusion of the healing of Jairus' daughter. He notes that she was 12 years old, the same number given for the years that the woman had suffered with her ailment.

The story opens with Jesus crossing from the Gentile east side of the Sea of Galilee to the Jewish west side. He is greeted by a prominent member of the village (presumably Capernaum), who acted as the leader of the synagogue, which indicates his social standing as well as his economic standing. Since synagogue meetings generally took place in a house during this part of the first century, the implication is that Jairus is well off. Nevertheless, like so many others, no amount of money can stem the tide of an illness for which there is no known cure.

When Jairus meets Jesus, Jairus' daughter is at the point of death. Matthew intensifies the drama of the story by saying that she had already died when Jairus approached Jesus. This minor disagreement is of little concern, since when Jesus arrives at Jairus' house all three accounts make it clear that the girl is dead. In approaching Jesus, Jairus expresses his belief in Jesus' power as a healer: "Come and lay your hands on her, so that she may be made well, and live" (Mark 5:23). Jesus responds favourably to this request and sets out for Jairus' house.

It is at this point in the story that a second ill person is introduced. A woman in the crowd is said to have been suffering from a hemorrhage for 12 years and "she had endured much under many physicians" (5:26). In antiquity, the available medical knowledge was not advanced and physicians had little or no knowledge about how a particular ailment began or how it might be cured. While we today might look to our own physicians for diagnosis and prescription, much of the ancient medical practice focused on description, with few remedies available to patients.

In this particular case, the woman has spent all of her money and is no closer to being better. In fact, her ailment has grown worse (5:26). This explains, in part, the woman's desperation. Upon hearing of Jesus she seeks him out and decides to make the bold step of getting close enough to touch his garment. To understand the full implications of this action, we must recall the plight of those who were ill in antiquity. Apart from the obvious discomfort of a physical illness, the illness itself was understood in the wider cultural context as an indication of God's displeasure with that person. As if this were not enough, there were clear regulations around where a woman could and could not be during her period of menstruation. Leviticus states that "When a woman has a discharge of blood that is her regular discharge from her body, she shall be in her impurity for seven days, and whoever touches her shall be unclean until the evening" (Leviticus 15:19). A woman for whom the flow of blood never ceased would remain in a permanent state of impurity (cf. Leviticus 15:25-30).

For the woman in our story, this state of impurity means that she has to endure not only physical discomfort but also social ostracism. It is likely that she is not welcome in her family's house or even in her home village due to others' fear of ritual pollution. She, like so many others that Jesus heals, lives on the margins of society. She is among the crowd on its way to Jairus' house, which suggests that she is not in her home village. If she were, she would be identified and chased away due to her uncleanness. A more likely scenario is that she has come from elsewhere to seek out healing from Jesus.

Seizing the moment, she reaches out to touch Jesus' garment. The narrator tells us what at this point in the Gospel should be no surprise – "immediately her hemorrhage stopped" (Mark

5:29). However, Jesus notices that he has been touched and stops to investigate. His words play off another common assumption in antiquity: miracles drain power from the healer. In this particular case, the disciples try to dispel the notion, pointing to the crowd, but Jesus persists. When the woman finally comes forward to confess her deed, a collective gasp would have been audible throughout the crowd. Some might already be bending down to pick up stones to throw at her. Those who witnessed what this woman had done would assume that she had rendered Jesus powerless. As a woman, she should not have touched a man; as a hemorrhaging woman, she would have made him ritually impure and rendered him powerless. This puts the life of Jairus' daughter in greater peril. The girl's only hope for life has disappeared in an instant through the selfish action of a woman who, after 12 years of illness, could not wait another hour to allow Jesus to heal Jairus' daughter.

Of course, we know that the woman's action will not affect Jesus, so it is strange that he should stop and take the time to seek her out. I imagine Jairus is getting increasingly frantic as Jesus scans the crowd. Jesus' response to the woman's confession is to proclaim, "Daughter, your faith has made you well" (5:34). More literally, this can be translated, "your faith has saved you." These words give the woman not physical healing – she already has that – but social healing. Jesus bears witness before the whole crowd that the woman is indeed free from the bondage of her ailment. The

61

people in her home village who may have been skeptical about her healing will be told that Jesus the healer affirmed the woman's "clean" state.

As we return to the original miracle story, that of Jairus' daughter, we find that Jairus' worst fears are realized. His little girl has died. Were Jesus one of the regular miracle workers of antiquity, the story would end here. However, Jesus is not a regular miracle worker. He continues to Jairus' house where, in the face of the derisive laughter of the attendants, he enters the girl's room and brings her back to life.

In this complex narrative we see clearly that Jesus' healing ministry goes well beyond overcoming physical ailments. Jesus shows concern for the whole person. It is not enough that the hemorrhaging woman should be healed; she needs to be fully integrated back into society. As we think about our own contexts we need to ask ourselves: Who are the people around us who are alienated due to some physical or mental ailment? Whom are we unwilling to include in our social circles? How would Jesus care for such people? What are we, therefore, called to do?

# 10

## The Gentile Woman's Daughter

"Even the dogs under the table
eat the children's crumbs."
Mark 7:24-30

The story of the healing of the Gentile woman's daughter is striking in its oddities. Inexplicably, Jesus departs from Galilee and walks northwest towards the coast, to the Gentile region of Tyre. One might think that he is taking a rest from his ministry, although his practice in such cases is to go out into the wilderness. His entering a house in the region of Tyre suggests that he is in a city or village. Immediately after this episode, Jesus returns to Galilee by way of Sidon and the region of the Decapolis (Mark 7:31). Since Sidon is north of Tyre, Jesus has taken a rather circuitous journey. As this is the only episode from that journey that is recorded in the Gospel, we must assume that it conveys an important lesson.

Whatever the reason for his journey, it is clear in Mark's account that Jesus hopes to remain incognito. Yet despite his efforts, a woman whose daughter is possessed by a demon discovers him. In the ensuing encounter between the woman and

Jesus, we see that she is a confident person. Mark tells us that the woman came to Jesus and begged him to exorcise the demon that had possession of her daughter. Matthew heightens the drama by recording her direct words: "Have mercy on me, Lord, Son of David; my daughter is tormented by a demon" (Matthew 15:22). What is striking here is that it is a woman, a mother, who approaches Jesus. In the patriarchal world of first-century CE Palestine, one would expect the *paterfamilias*, the male head of the household, to approach Jesus with the request. This was the case with Jairus, the ruler of the synagogue at Capernaum, whose daughter was ill. In the first century CE, women were not to approach men outside their family except through a male intermediary.

Matthew's telling of the story heightens the social problems of a woman approaching a male. In Matthew's account, Jesus "did not answer her at all" (Matthew 15:23). This would not, at that time, be perceived as an insult: Jesus was acting properly and according to custom. The fact that she is a Gentile makes the situation more difficult for Jesus. As a Jew he would be expected to have nothing to do with her, lest he become unclean. In Matthew we hear of the disciples' remedy for the situation: "Send her away, for she keeps shouting after us" (Matthew 15:23). When Jesus does answer it is to rebuff her; he tells her that he was sent only for the Jewish people. The situation conspires against this Gentile woman. Her only hope for her demon-possessed daughter is a Jewish man from another region, but he refuses to help her.

Jesus attempts to drive her away, saying, "Let the children be fed first, for it is not fair to take the children's food and throw it to the dogs" (Mark 7:27). For Jews, dogs were synonymous with "unclean," and the term was used by Jews to describe those outside the covenant. For Gentiles, dogs were associated with such unpleasant characteristics as greed, fawning and shamelessness. It seems as if Jesus is insulting this Gentile woman. The point is one of contrast: unlike the chosen people of God, all others are scavengers. The woman is not deterred. In her confidence she accepts the comparison and makes it her own. Admitting to be a "dog" she notes that even dogs eat what the children drop under the table. She is not asking to be included in the family. She only asks that she might have the scraps.

Again, Matthew makes clear what is only implied in Mark's account. When the woman first approaches Jesus she asks him, "Have mercy on *me*," and then points to her demon-possessed daughter. Since she approaches without a male guardian she is likely already outside the community. Her daughter's condition would bring suspicion upon her and her household. With no husband to act on behalf of the family, and no brother or uncle willing to take up her cause, she must fend for herself. In asking for mercy on "me" she is signalling to Jesus that she is the centre of a family of disrepute. Her situation is already desperate; the insults of a Jewish rabbi are nothing to be feared. Having nothing to lose, she boldly approaches Jesus and demands his assistance. Taking on the role of a male, she enters into debate with the visiting rabbi, determined to show him how worthy is her cause.

In the final scene, Jesus relents and acts upon her request. In Mark, he responds to the wit of her remark about dogs under the table: "For saying that you may go – the demon has left your daughter" (Mark 7:29). However, Matthew makes it clear that it was not her wit alone but her faith that swayed Jesus: "Woman, great is your faith! Let it be done for you as you wish" (Matthew 15:28). The woman shows her confidence in a third and final act – she immediately leaves Jesus and returns home to her daughter. She does not insist that Jesus return home with her to make sure her daughter is truly healed. She needs no special touch or incantations. Jesus has spoken and she believes the deed has been accomplished.

The faith of the Gentile woman is exemplary. It is unaffected by outward situations; cultural taboos do not prevent her from approaching Jesus. Jesus' initial negative response to her request does not deter her. Her faith in Jesus' ability to heal her daughter, and thus heal her own situation, is evident in her bold, confident approach. In our prayer life, we need to speak to God as the Gentile woman did: boldly, confidently, even argumentatively. Grounded firmly in our belief in God's ability to act on our behalf, we can approach the throne of grace with full confidence that God hears our requests.

# 11

# The Blind Man at Bethsaida

"I can see people, but they
look like trees, walking."
Mark 8:22-26

The healing of the blind man at Bethsaida (Mark 8:22-26) and the healing of the deaf person with a speech impediment (Mark 7:32-37) are the only miracles where Jesus is described as employing some of the physical elements commonly used by healers in antiquity. In the healing of the deaf person with a speech impediment, Jesus places his fingers in the man's ears, spits and touches the man's tongue. In the healing of the blind man, Jesus places his own saliva on the man's eyes before laying his hands upon him.

It is interesting to note that Matthew and Luke did not include the stories of the blind man at Bethsaida and the healing of the deaf person with a speech impediment in their accounts of Jesus' ministry, even though they had both read Mark's Gospel account. It is probable that Matthew and Luke saw Jesus' powers as very different from, and much greater than, those of the magicians who travel the world. To highlight the fact that Jesus was different from these healers, they leave out the two exceptional cases in which Jesus uses physical elements in his healing. In the case of the healing of the blind man, the oddness of the story itself may have made Matthew and Luke hesitate to include it in their accounts. Jesus' first actions only partially heal the man: "I can see people, but they look like trees, walking" (Mark 8:24). Jesus then has to touch the man a second time to fully restore his sight. In all the other healings Jesus does, the healing takes place immediately upon the first actions of Jesus. Realizing that some readers might mistakenly think that Jesus was not powerful enough to accomplish the healing the first time, Matthew and Luke may have decided to omit it.

So why did Mark consider this story worth including in his Gospel? Biblical scholars have long identified a twofold structure to Mark's Gospel. The first half focuses on Jesus' identity, addressing the question "Who is this man?" Clearly, the answer is "Jesus is the Christ, the Son of God," an identification given in the very first verse of the Gospel (Mark 1:1). The second half of Mark's Gospel turns its attention to the issue "What does he do?" The answer is "The Christ must suffer, die and rise," a message that is repeated three times (8:31; 9:30-32; 10:32-34). The turning point in Mark is Peter's confession (8:27-30), where he declares to Jesus: "You are the Messiah" (8:29). In response, Jesus teaches the disciples that "The Son of Man must undergo great suffering, and be rejected by the elders, the chief priests, and the scribes, and be killed, and after three days rise again" (8:31). Yet, despite Peter's correct identification of Jesus as the Messiah, he responds to Jesus' task by rebuking Jesus for conceiving of his mission in this way.

Peter's dual response in this passage is fairly typical of his actions throughout the Gospel. He partly understands Jesus' identity and mission, but the details elude him. It is only after Jesus' death and resurrection that Peter is able to understand fully. And here is the connection to the miraculous healing of the blind man: for Mark, it serves as an illustration of the process of understanding that the disciples undergo. Mark places this healing story immediately after a discourse in which Jesus warns the disciples about his opponents. They mistake his warning, thinking he is criticizing them for forgetting to bring bread. In response, Jesus reminds them of the feeding miracles and asks, "Do you have eyes, and fail to see? Do you have ears, and fail to hear?" (Mark 8:18). The disciples seem to be blind!

On the other side of the story of the healing of the blind man is Peter's confession of who Jesus is and what he has come to do. Like the blind man who receives the gift of sight in two stages, so Peter, along with the other disciples, comes to a full understanding of and belief in Jesus in two stages. Until the disciples witness Jesus' death and resurrection, they "see" only as the blind man first sees – vague images that seem right but are poorly defined.

Another important element might have informed Mark's decision to include this miracle alongside the healing of the deaf person with a speech impediment. Together, these miracles suggest a fulfillment of Isaiah's description of the final days of God's salvation: "Then the eyes of the blind shall be opened, and the ears of the deaf unstopped; then the lame shall leap like a deer, and the tongue of the speechless sing for joy" (Isaiah 35:5-6). These healings are part of the larger in-breaking of the kingdom of God through the life and ministry of Jesus.

Mark uses this miracle to remind us of how important it is for us as disciples to understand who Jesus is and what his mission is about. The miracle reminds us that the kingdom of God has broken into the world and God is active among us. We must choose how to respond. Are we like Peter, who pays lip-service to Jesus but would prevent him from doing God's will? Or are we like Peter who, having fully experienced the risen Jesus, boldly proclaims the kingdom of God?

# 12

## The Spirit-Possessed Boy

"I believe; help my unbelief!"
Mark 9:14-29

The father in this miracle story expresses the desperate cry that many of us have felt at one time or another in our faith journey: "I believe; help my unbelief!" (Mark 9:24). On the surface, the cry is a contradiction. If he believes, there is no need to help his unbelief. If he does not believe, how can he claim to believe? The ambiguity of the statement is intriguing. Many who have followed Christ for years find there are times when their faith wanes. Often circumstances conspire to challenge what we thought to be a deep-seated belief in God.

This man's circumstances have done just that. His son has a condition that causes him to have seizures in which he falls down, sometimes into fire or water, foams at the mouth, grinds his teeth and becomes rigid. In other words, he acts outside the boundaries of what was considered at that time to be normal. Many interpreters suggest that the boy seems to have epilepsy. The translators of the NRSV Bible even use the term "epileptic" to describe the boy's condition (Matthew 17:15).

However, this term would not have been used 2,000 years ago. The word Matthew uses can be translated literally as "moonstruck." Yet, as with all illnesses, his condition is thought to be due to a spirit that possesses him.

The man was no doubt overjoyed at the birth of his son. In antiquity, sons were highly prized as they would carry on the family name through their own families. However, for this man the joy turns to despair as the boy begins to show symptoms of his condition. Luke notes that the boy is this man's only child (Luke 9:38). Since his son would not be able to marry due to his illness, the father faced the end of his family line. In addition, the family's place in the village was threatened; the entire community would ostracize a man with a demon-possessed son. In our culture, we tend to be identified by what we do, particularly our occupation and our hobbies. In antiquity, a person was more apt to be identified by their family connections. In greeting someone, one would inquire about a person's extended family, clan and place of residence. Thus, the son's illness threatens the man's sense of self. How will he be remembered by the generations to come? No wonder the man's faith in God is wavering.

On the other hand, the man has not given up all hope. Having found the disciples of Jesus, even without Jesus present, he has asked them to heal his son. Already the disciples are becoming known for their healing ministry, and this man believes that they can heal his son. However, the task proves to be beyond their abilities and they are unable to heal him. It is at this point that Jesus enters the story. Returning from the mountain after his Transfiguration, he finds the scribes and his disciples arguing. Although nothing is said about the reason for the argument, it likely concerns the disciples' inability to heal as evidence for the lack of divine sanction upon them and their master.

It is the father of the sick boy who first addresses Jesus directly. Despite the disciples' inability to heal his son, the father approaches Jesus quickly in order to tell him what is happening. Jesus' response is interesting: "You faithless generation, how much longer must I be among you? How much longer must I put up with you?" (Mark 9:19). It seems at first that Jesus is directing his critique at the man himself. However, the Greek word "you" here is plural. Thus, the man, the disciples, the scribes, and even the whole crowd are implicated in Jesus' question. Jesus is not challenging their belief around this particular miracle, but their reluctance to recognize the full implications of his ministry. The miracles that he performs there are not for entertainment or to give solace to a few individuals. Jesus' miracles are signs that the kingdom of God has broken into the world. And yet, these people still cannot recognize that it has arrived. Jesus seems to suggest that had they done so, their collective faith would have been an effective weapon against the spirit thought to be possessing the boy.

The father continues his conversation with Jesus by describing the boy's affliction. He concludes by begging Jesus, "If you are able to do anything, have pity on us and help us" (9:22). The father's request is not simply for the boy but for the whole family: "help *us*." As we have seen in other miracles, Jesus' concern is not just for physical health, but for the whole person. In this case, the whole person extends beyond the boy to his entire family. Jesus' incredulity is evident in his response. To paraphrase, he says, "You ask if I am able – ha!" He shifts the question to the man, who clearly does not truly understand who Jesus is, unlike the others who have come to Jesus and whose faith, Jesus says, has made them well. Jesus points out that the man need only believe. Nevertheless, the man has had belief enough to request Jesus' help for his son and so responds, "I believe." He now realizes his own need for deeper faith and says to Jesus, "Help my unbelief." He asks Jesus to address the underlying state that would cause him to question why God would allow such a thing to happen to his family.

The concluding private discussion between Jesus and his disciples highlights the role of faith in the healing miracles. When the disciples ask him why they could not cast out this spirit, Jesus answers, "This kind can come out only through prayer" (9:29). There are different kinds of demonic spirits; greater faith is needed for the disciples to be able to bring about the healing. Jesus, it is interesting to note, does not pray when casting out the spirit, showing that he has powers greater than the disciples can ever attain.

This miracle story illustrates the effect of faith, and unbelief, on Christian activities of all kinds. It is not a matter of figuring out which activities demand more intense prayer. Rather, the constant wrestling between belief and unbelief that characterizes the life of faith demands that all our activities be shrouded in prayer. Prayer allows us to focus our attention on the true source of the power that enables the Christian life: "The kingdom, the power and the glory be yours," as we pray in the doxology after the Lord's Prayer. Through prayer, we seek what God would have us do: "Your will be done." Through prayer, we realize that our life is to be an enactment of our prayer: "Your kingdom come." As we look to God to accompany us on our faith journey, and to help us overcome our unbelief, we need to heed Paul's exhortation to "Pray without ceasing" (1 Thessalonians 5:17).

# 13

## The Withering of the Fig Tree

"Have faith in God."
Mark 11:12-14, 20-25

In the last of the pre-resurrection miracles to occur in Mark's Gospel, a nature miracle, Jesus shows his power over the created world. However, in this instance – the withering of the fig tree – the miracle is not the focus of the story. Rather, the miracle is an object lesson that illustrates the power of Christian prayer, and links this power to Christian forgiveness of others. There are indications that the event is to be understood as a symbolic prophetic action.

When Jesus approaches Jerusalem from the village of Bethany, where he had spent the night before, he is hungry and so explores the offerings of a fig tree along the road. Finding it barren of fruit he says, in what seems to be a fit of rage, "May no one ever eat fruit from you again" (Mark 11:14). It is an odd reaction, particularly since, as Mark points out, it was not the season for figs. It seems strange, as well, that the lack of fruit would disappoint Jesus when he could perhaps satisfy his hunger through a different sort of miracle. After all, this is the person who fed 5,000 and then 4,000 people with a few loaves and fish! Why not force the tree to bring forth food that instant? Jesus' reaction tells us there is more going on in this story than meets the eye.

In Mark's Gospel, the miracle is presented in two parts. After pronouncing the curse on the fig tree, Jesus continues on his way to Jerusalem, where he drives out the merchants from the temple. The disciples do not seem to notice the fig tree on their way back to Bethany, but the next day, as they travel again to Jerusalem, they discover that it is withered to its roots.

Matthew's account of the same miracle is somewhat different (the miracle does not occur in Luke). In Matthew, Jesus curses the fig tree and "the fig tree withered at once" (Matthew 21:19). The immediacy of the withering emphasizes Jesus' power and gives Jesus the opportunity to highlight the power of prayer. The prevailing assumption is that Matthew integrates the two-stage miracle of Mark, lest Mark's version be taken as indicative of a less powerful Jesus whose miracles take time to be effective. But the latter perspective is unlikely to be Mark's view, since in so many other instances Jesus' miracles have been immediate. Again, we need to ask why Mark presents this miracle in this way.

In Mark's narrative the two stages of the cursing of the fig tree bracket the account of the cleansing of the temple (Mark 11:15-19). Each of these actions is prophetic; each carries with it some symbolism of a greater reality. God often calls prophets to undertake symbolic actions. Isaiah walks naked for three years (Isaiah 20:1-6), Jeremiah smashes a pot (Jeremiah 19:1-13), Ezekiel cuts his hair (Ezekiel 5:1-4) and Hosea marries a prostitute (Hosea 1:2-3). Jesus' action of driving the merchants out of the temple symbolizes a time when temple sacrifice will no longer be necessary for communication with God. The withering of the fig tree symbolizes the temple, which appears to be in a stage of healthy growth (green leaves) but upon closer inspection does not even have the green buds of fruit. As the tree is destroyed, so shall be the temple. However, the fig tree points beyond the temple, symbolizing the future of those who would claim to follow God but do not produce fruit that shows their relationship with God.

The temple in Jerusalem was the central focus of early first-century CE Jewish worship. Herod the Great, for all his faults, was a keen builder, and he committed much time and money to building the elaborate temple. (The rebuilding began circa 20/19 BCE and was completed circa 63 CE. It was destroyed with the rest of Jerusalem seven years later during the Jewish war against the Romans [66–70 CE].) The temple was a colossal structure with an outer porch, a courtyard for the Gentiles, an inner courtyard for women, and an innermost sanctuary where stood the holy of holies, the place of the yearly sacrifice for sin. The temple building itself served as the central bank, complete with safety deposit boxes. Hence, when Jesus turned over the tables in the temple it was a significant gesture. It was like trashing the main branch of a bank or knocking out the computers at a stock exchange – it was a challenge to the economic system as well as to the religious authorities.

When Jesus accuses the people of turning the temple into a "den of robbers," he is alluding to the prophet Jeremiah's accusation against worshippers who desecrate the temple by their idolatry and lawlessness (Jeremiah 7:11). Jeremiah warned the priests of his time that the temple had become a den of thieves and prophesied that God would destroy the Jerusalem sanctuary as God had done at Shiloh. Later, Zechariah, prophesying against the background of the post-exilic temple, would promise that on the day of the Lord all would be holy in Jerusalem and no merchant would be found in the temple (Zechariah 14:21). Jesus' action should be seen as a prophetic protest against the desecration of God's house and a sign that the messianic purification of the temple is at hand.

Returning to Jerusalem the day after the cleansing of the temple, the disciples find the fig tree withered. Jesus explains the significance of his symbolic action: if the disciples have complete faith in God, anything is possible. Jesus even points to the mountain upon which they stand, the Mount of Olives, and suggests that with true faith they could move it into the sea. Yes, this is hyperbole: it is meant to show that no matter how big the task, God will answer the prayers of God's people. Indeed, in praying one must believe that the prayer has already been answered. Jesus curses the fig tree in the belief that the curse will take effect. Sure enough, the next day the disciples note that it has happened. But for Jesus, the withering happened the instant the words left his mouth. From that moment there was little hope for the tree, since he knew God would answer his prayer-curse.

The final saying balances what might otherwise be a judgmental attitude. Jesus' caveat about prayer is that it must include forgiveness: "Whenever you stand praying, forgive, if you have anything against anyone; so that your Father in heaven may also forgive you your trespasses" (Mark 11:25). God stands in judgment over us; we are not to judge one another. Like those in the temple whom Jesus drives out, we are called to examine our actions and our attitudes to see whether they conform to the will of God. If they do not, if we do not bear the fruit of the good works to which we are called, and if we stand in judgment over others, then like the fig tree we will wither and die spiritually. Like the merchants in the temple, we will be driven out from the presence of God.

# 14

## The Large Catch of Fish

"Go away from me, Lord,
for I am a sinful man!"
Luke 5:1-11

As those who make their living in the fishing industry know, it can be a frustrating occupation. Some days the fish are plentiful; other days there is scarcely a fish to be found. Nevertheless, whatever the day's results, the fisher folk prepare their nets and their boats for the next day's work. In the story of the large catch of fish, Jesus meets some fishermen on the shore of the Sea of Galilee. Their day of fishing, which began before dawn, proved fruitless. Having returned to the shore with nothing to show for their work, they spread their nets out on the rocky beach to wash away the weeds that had been caught in them.

Luke's account of the calling of Simon Peter differs somewhat from Matthew's and Mark's accounts. The setting is the same: Peter is a fisherman whom Jesus encounters on the shore of the Sea of Galilee. In all three Gospels, Jesus explains to Peter and his friends that in following him they will be fishing for people. In Matthew and Mark there is no miracle associated with the calling and Peter expresses no resistance. The extra details Luke provides, however, show clearly that this is more than a chance encounter. It has all the markings of a divine call story.

The Bible contains a number of stories about God calling people to a specific task. These calls include five discernible steps: God appears; the person being called expresses fear or doubt about the calling; a heavenly message is given; the one being called objects; and the person is given a sign of reassurance about the calling.

Take, for example, the story of God calling Moses to lead the Israelites out of bondage. First, a messenger of the Lord appears in a flame of fire in a bush that is not consumed (Exodus 3:2). Second, Moses expresses fear or doubt about the calling – "Moses hid his face, for he was afraid to look at God" (3:6). Third, the heavenly message commissions Moses to go to Pharaoh and demand the release of the Hebrews (3:10). Fourth, Moses expresses an objection – "Who am I that I should go to Pharaoh, and bring the Israelites out of Egypt?" (3:11). Finally, Moses receives a sign of reassurance that confirms the divine calling: the revelation of the divine name (3:14) and the turning of his staff into a snake (4:3).

Although these five elements of a divine call story do not always appear in this order, they are all there. When Gideon is called, the signs begin with the appearance of a messenger of the Lord who greets him with the words "The Lord is with you" (Judges 6:12; appearance). Gideon is skeptical and asks, "If the Lord is with us, why then has all this happened to us?" (6:13; doubt). The messenger does not answer the question but instead commissions Gideon to deliver Israel from its Midianite oppressors (6:14; commission). In response, Gideon points out his weakness and his low status within his tribe and his family (6:15; objection). He then asks for a sign of reassurance, which he receives through the miraculous consumption of a meat and cake offering that he prepares (6:17-24; sign).

We find all the elements of a divine call story in Luke's account of the miraculous catch of fish. The narrative opens with the appearance of Jesus, who has already been clearly identified as a messenger of God through his miraculous birth, his resistance to temptation and his inaugural sermon in Nazareth. After teaching the crowds from a boat, he asks Peter and the others to put out from shore and let down their nets. After a fruitless morning of fishing these seasoned fishermen would likely have scoffed at Jesus' amateurish idea of catching fish in the heat of the day, when the fish have descended to the coolness of the lake bottom. Peter expresses his skepticism to Jesus but agrees to go ahead anyway (Luke 5:6). In this call story, the sign of reassurance is given before the commission. The nets that are let down suddenly overflow with fish (5:6-7). Although Jesus gives no word or signal that he has performed a miracle, the fishermen know that this catch would have been unlikely without divine intervention. Peter's response is an objection: "Go away from me, Lord, for I am a sinful man!" (5:8).

Finally, Jesus gives the commission itself: "Do not be afraid; from now on you will be catching people" (5:10). When they get back to shore, the fishermen leave their nets and their boats and take up the commission to follow Jesus and be involved in his ministry.

Despite the inclusion of a sign of reassurance in these and other call stories, there is no guarantee that the one called will sustain the commitment. In the Gospels, Peter often seems unsure of his calling. He misunderstands Jesus' teachings, questions Jesus' own description of his mission, and eventually denies that he even knows Jesus. In the First Testament, Moses is in constant need of God's reassurance (Exodus 4:6-8, 10-17; 5:22–6:9; 6:28–7:5) and Gideon needs to put out a fleece not once but twice (Judges 6:36-40).

Jesus calls us to follow him. Many of us will have moments of doubt about what we are called to do. Like others called before us, we must carry on, looking for signs of reassurance that God sends our way. As the apostle Paul says:

I want to know Christ and the power of his resurrection and the sharing of his sufferings by becoming like him in his death, if somehow I may attain the resurrection from the dead. Not that I have already obtained this or have already reached the goal; but I press on to make it my own, because Christ Jesus has made me his own. Beloved, I do not consider that I have made it my own; but this one thing I do: forgetting what lies behind and straining forward to what lies ahead, I press on toward the goal for the prize of the heavenly call of God in Christ Jesus (Philippians 3:10-14).

Following Jesus is like fishing: it has its good days and its bad days. What sustains us through it all is knowing that our calling is grounded in the divine will of God.

# *15*

# Resuscitating a Widow's Son

"Do not weep."
Luke 7:11-17

As a result of his miracles, Jesus' reputation spread around Galilee. People began to ask who was this man who could perform such wonders. Later in the Gospel narrative we learn that the crowds proposed various possibilities, such as "prophet" or "John the Baptist revived from the dead." Some even suggested that Jesus was working in the tradition of the prophet Elijah (Luke 9:19). This viewpoint originated with the raising of the widow's son from the dead. In this miracle there are clear connections between Jesus and the prophet Elijah.

The town of Nain is approximately 9 kilometres (5.5 miles) southeast of Nazareth. As Jesus approaches this town he meets a funeral procession carrying a man on a stretcher. Among the mourners is the man's mother, who we discover is a widow. The deceased man is her only son, and although he is no longer a child, she is close to him. The love of a mother for her son is understandable in any culture. However, in antiquity this woman's connection to her son goes beyond the bond of motherhood. Under Roman law and Jewish custom, all but a few women were required to have a male guardian, called a *kyrios*, who would take care of them. This *kyrios* was charged with providing for the woman and conducting financial and legal transactions on her behalf. Typically, the role of *kyrios* fell upon the woman's father or husband, depending on her marital status. When neither was present, the task was taken up by her closest living male relative – often her eldest son.

Without the social and legal protection of a *kyrios* a woman became quite vulnerable. Unable to work outside her own home due to the social restrictions on women, she had little opportunity to earn a living and little to offer the village. The one possibility that was open to her was prostitution, and even that would not be feasible if she was over a certain age. Such is the plight of the widow in this story. Her only son, her *kyrios*, has died and she no longer has anyone to care for her.

When Jesus meets this woman at the town gate, he has compassion on her. It is noteworthy that his compassion is not for the one who has died but for the one who is left behind. More significant, perhaps, is the way Luke refers to Jesus here. Whereas in most of Luke's miracle accounts he notes that "Jesus" speaks or acts, in this particular case he designates Jesus with the word "Lord" – "When the Lord saw her" (Luke 7:13). In Greek, the word used here and translated as "Lord" is *kyrios*. It is as if Luke wants to signal to his readers that

Jesus has quickly understood the widow's plight and designated himself as her guardian.

He will not hold this position for long, however. Touching the stretcher, Jesus commands, "Young man, I say to you, rise!" (v. 14). The man does get up, and even speaks in order to show the crowd that he really lives. Jesus' next action is equally important: "Jesus gave him to his mother" (7:15). In so doing, Jesus transfers the responsibility of *kyrios* from himself back to the son. The son is brought back to life and can now care for his mother, securing for her a continued place in the life of the village. By restoring her son to life, Jesus restores her hope for the future. As is typical in his ministry, Jesus cares for a person of insecure social standing and reintegrates her into society.

As important as this lesson is, the story points beyond the immediate situation to a much greater truth through its connections with the story of Elijah's healing of a widow's son (1 Kings 17:8-24). This comparison is made in the story itself when the crowd proclaims, "A great prophet has risen among us!" (Luke 7:16). Elijah was considered a "great prophet," perhaps the greatest. He is usually linked with Moses as representing the Law and the Prophets. For this reason, the two appear with Jesus in the transfiguration account (Luke 9:28-36). (Elijah's service to God did not end with his death but with his being taken up into heaven in a chariot of fire [2 Kings 2:11].) During his ministry, Elijah stayed with a Gentile woman in Zarephath (1 Kings 17:8-24). In the course of his stay, the widow's only son falls ill and dies. As a result of her appeal to him, Elijah petitions God and the son is brought back to life. As in the case of Jesus' miracle, this action restores not only the life of the son but also the future of the mother.

Jesus' action and its connection with the action of Elijah take us back to Jesus' inaugural proclamation in Nazareth. After reading from the Scriptures in the synagogue service, Jesus announces that he is the one who will bring about the time of the jubilee. The First Testament records that every fiftieth year will be a jubilee year. During the jubilee year, the land is to be given a rest from sowing, reaping and harvesting, financial debts are to be cancelled, and slaves set free (see Leviticus 25). Jesus announces that he will now bring about the jubilee by bringing liberty and release to those who are bound by physical or social circumstances (Luke 4:17-21).

Jesus goes on to point out that both Elijah and Elisha did not minister to those in Israel but instead were sent to Gentiles (4:25-26). Elijah provided an unending supply of food to the Gentile widow and brought her son back to life (1 Kings 17:8-16), while Elisha healed Naaman, the Syrian army officer, of leprosy (2 Kings 5:1-14). Their actions anticipate Jesus' concern for Gentiles (cf. Mark 7:24-30) and at the same time show that Jesus' ministry is linked to that of Elijah.

Like Elijah, Jesus notes the concerns of a widow. Luke extends this message to show that Christians should care for widows. Widows are mentioned in Luke's second volume, the Book of

Acts, as a group within the early Church that receive special attention (Acts 6:1). Other Second Testament and early Christian writings reveal that widows formed an important sector of the early Church. Early Christians took it upon themselves to care for those women who had no one else to care for them. Today, it is not necessarily widows who are in need of our care, nor is it necessarily only women. However, there remains a pressing need for Christians to minister to those who have no one to look after them. This could mean restoring broken relationships, just as Elijah and Jesus restored the widows' relationships with their sons. Restoration, like raising someone from the dead, brings people to new life and new possibilities for growth. This, too, is part of our ministry of healing.

# 16

## The Bent-over Woman

"You are set free from your ailment."
Luke 13:10-17

The healing of the bent-over woman follows
Jesus' discussion of two examples of death:
Galileans who have been brutalized at the hands of
Pilate and others who perished in the accidental
collapse of a tower (Luke 13:1-4). Jesus offers a dire
warning in response: "Unless you repent, you will
all perish just as they did" (v. 5). He then tells the
parable of the barren fig tree that is under threat of
the axe unless it bears good fruit.

Since illness was linked to sin, a woman "bound
by Satan" for 18 years would have been viewed as
having committed grievous sins for which she was
justly punished. However, Jesus once again goes
against cultural expectations. While teaching in the
synagogue, he notices that the woman is unable to
stand up straight. For 18 years, about half of her
lifespan, she has had to walk in a stooped position.
While the pain of such a position would be almost
unbearable, the social implications made things
even worse. In antiquity, the physical position of
being bent-over symbolized the position of a slave.

Jobs that required stooping went to the slaves of little consequence. Thus, this woman is suffering from both physical and social distress.

When he sees this woman Jesus calls her over and proclaims, "Woman, you are set free from your ailment" (v. 12). His language is carefully chosen. Jesus addresses the perceived cause of the ailment – Satan's bondage. In healing this woman by freeing her from this bondage Jesus once again shows his place in the divine hierarchy. Although Satan's power is great, it is no match for Jesus. Later, in the midst of controversy over her healing, Jesus will affirm that the woman is "a daughter of Abraham" (v. 16), signalling that she has a place in the mainstream of society. Now that she is no longer physically ill, she may be reintegrated socially.

Since this action is performed on the Sabbath, an argument with the Pharisees ensues. Unlike Jesus' other Sabbath healings, the physical healing is completed before the controversy begins. Jesus' response to the Pharisees is typical of Jewish reasoning. Jesus points out that his accusers are quite willing to unbind a domestic animal on the Sabbath day. How much greater, he implies, is the necessity to unbind a woman bound by Satan. Later rabbinic tradition would deem such argumentation *qal vahomer*, from the lighter instance to the heavier instance. Jesus' actions represent an in-breaking of the kingdom of God on the day reserved for God. There is no tension between the work of healing and the holiness of the Sabbath. Both represent the kingdom of God among us and are fully compatible. The welfare of a human being takes precedence over obligations placed upon us by religious institutions.

One of the more striking aspects of this healing story is the repetition of the number 18. Numbers in biblical writings often have a deeper significance: for example, the number 7 represents perfection while the infamous 666 is the number of the beast (Revelation 13:18). But the number 18 does not seem to have any particular significance. The only other use of the number 18 in the Second Testament occurs immediately before this healing, when we are told that 18 people were killed in the collapse of the tower at Siloam (Luke 13:4), a connection that is probably coincidental. But can we make anything of the 18 years of suffering the woman endured? We mentioned earlier that she probably suffered with the ailment for half her life. But does the number 18 have any other connections?

The First Testament is the obvious place to look, since it is a frequent source of quotations and allusions for the Gospel writers. The book of Judges records that the Israelites served King Eglon of Moab for 18 years "because they had done what was evil in the sight of the LORD" (Judges 3:12-14). However, "when the Israelites cried out to the LORD, the LORD raised up for them a deliverer, Ehud son of Gera, the Benjaminite, a left-handed man" (Judges 3:15), who killed King Eglon and led the Israelites into triumph over the Moabite army. Judges 10:7-8 records that God's anger against Israel's idolatry was so great that he turned them over to the Ammonites. "For eighteen years they oppressed all the Israelites," both those in their own land and those in the land of Canaan (Judges 10:8). After 18 years of oppression at the hands of the Ammonites the Israelites put away their false gods and properly worshipped God. As a result, God raised up among them Jephthah, who went on to defeat the Ammonites (Judges 11:1-33).

The history of Israel recorded in 1 Kings tells of how the land secured by David and Solomon became divided into two nations: Israel, led by Jeroboam; and Judah, led by Rehoboam (1 Kings 12). After 18 oppressive years of King Rehoboam's reign (cf. 1 Kings 15:1), his son ascended to the throne. Although King Abijam was not much better as a ruler of Judah, for the sake of his ancestor David "God gave him a lamp in Jerusalem, setting up his son after him, and establishing Jerusalem" (1 Kings 15:4). Some stability was brought to the southern kingdom despite the sinfulness of its king.

A much better king came along much later. In his eighteenth year, Josiah successfully reinstated Passover observance, which had not been kept since before the kingdom of Israel was founded (2 Kings 23:22). At the same time, "Josiah put away the mediums, wizards, teraphim, idols, and all the abominations that were seen in the land of Judah and in Jerusalem" in order to re-establish God's presence in the land (2 Kings 23:24).

Finally, in the eighteenth year of the Babylonian king Nebuchadrezzar (Jeremiah 32:1), the great prophet Jeremiah received word that God would liberate the Judeans from bondage. Jeremiah is commanded to purchase a field in Judah in anticipation of a time when the land will be free from the Babylonian overlords (32:6). In the same cycle of visions God tells Jeremiah:

> The days are surely coming, says the LORD, when I will fulfill the promise I made to the house of Israel and the house of Judah. In those days and at that time I will cause a righteous Branch to spring up for David; and he shall execute justice and righteousness in the land (Jeremiah 33:14-15).

Christians later understood this passage to refer to Jesus.

In each of the cases listed above, which are the only cases in the First Testament where "18 years" is designated, that "18 years" is a time of oppression of Israel by a foreign power. During the eighteenth year, God steps in to free his people from bondage to a foreign or corrupt king.

Let us return to the healing of the bent-over woman. We note that the length of her own bondage to the power of Satan is mentioned twice. It is reasonable to suggest that Luke wants to highlight for those who know the history of Israel that the time has come for her to be released. This may be why Jesus follows this healing story with the parable of the mustard seed (Luke 13:18-19). In it, the kingdom of God is compared favourably to a small seed that grows like a weed throughout good farmland, polluting it along the way (cf. Leviticus 19:19; Deuteronomy 22:9-11). The healing of the marginalized woman represents the in-breaking of the kingdom of God. God no longer chooses powerful judges, kings and prophets to bring an end to bondage. Now, the kingdom is brought about through a Galilean peasant who will die an ignoble death.

# 17

## The Man with Dropsy

"All who exalt themselves will be humbled."
Luke 14:1-24

In Chapter 14 of his Gospel, Luke records a meal that Jesus shares with one of the leaders of the Pharisees. As both a leader and a Pharisee, the man likely is quite wealthy and moves in powerful circles. He invites Jesus and some other Pharisees to dine with him.

Meals, like all other aspects of first-century CE life, were governed by certain social rules. Where a person sat was a statement of social relations and reflected everyday social standing. Guests of lower social rank, if invited at all, were often assigned to different rooms and even served different food and wine. Indeed, the Gospels (especially Luke's) are full of references to behaviour at meals: whether one washes (Luke 11:38); who eats what, when and where (Luke 6:4); what is done or fails to get done at the table (Luke 7:38, 40, 44, 49); who is invited (Luke 14:12-14); where people sit (Luke 14:7-11); with whom one eats (Luke 15:2); and in what order persons of different rank come to the table (Luke 17:7-8). Before Jesus even arrives at the house of the

Pharisee, the other Pharisees are "watching him closely" (Luke 14:1), scrutinizing his actions to see whether he is worthy to be in their company. Already they are aware that Jesus is not like them or like anyone else in his understanding of Torah.

As Jesus approaches the Pharisee's house, he comes across a man with dropsy and heals him. (This is the only place in the Bible where dropsy is mentioned.) The healing episode fades into the background almost immediately and seems somewhat out of place. Unlike on most occasions in which Jesus does something controversial, in this instance the Pharisees are surprisingly silent. However, this little miracle frames the entire episode described in Luke 14:1-24 and is an important starting point for placing Jesus' teaching in context.

As Willi Braun points out in his book *Feasting and Social Rhetoric in Luke 14*,[3] the emphasis in this passage is on the man's condition. Therein lies the significance of the story. The condition labelled here as "dropsy" causes swelling of the body (primarily the arms and legs) due to excessive fluids in the body. Today this is more commonly known as edema. People who have edema find that it causes an unquenchable thirst and insatiable hunger. The continual storage of fluids, with little means to expel them, can lead to further complications and, if left untreated, death.

Although dropsy was a real and dangerous disease in antiquity, the condition became a metaphor for the moral condition of a person. The Cynic philosophers, who provided counter-cultural voices in antiquity, saw it in this light. The Cynics did not own possessions and wandered from place to place proclaiming their message of simplicity and freedom from material goods. They saw dropsy as a metaphor for people who have an abundance of wealth but have an unquenchable craving for more. Diogenes, one of the earliest Cynics, compared money-lovers to persons with dropsy:

> As dropsies though filled with fluid crave drink, so money-lovers, though loaded with money, crave more of it, yet both to their demise. For, their desires increase the more they acquire the objects of their cravings.[4]

For the Cynics, dropsy was a symptom of the addiction to luxury. In a similar fashion, the Roman poet Horace notes the link between the symptoms of dropsy and a lust for material possessions. Horace suggests that the greedy person heed the advice of those who recommend simplicity: "If you were troubled by thirst that no water could quench, you would tell your doctor about it; then if, with possessions amassed you feel only cravings for more, would you fail to take counsel with someone about it?"[5] Such comparisons are found in other writers, too, including Plutarch, Seneca and Ovid. Ovid writes:

> So he whose belly swells with dropsy, the more he drinks, the thirstier he grows. Nowadays nothing but money counts: fortune brings honours, friendships; the poor man everywhere lies low.[6]

The use of dropsy as a metaphor for unsatiated consumption was common in the first century CE. Novelists and playwrights often played with the double meaning of the term "dropsy," which suggests that even the non-elite members of society would have been familiar with the metaphor through their popular entertainment. The metaphor itself reflects upon those who are greedy, who love money, and who are involved in excessive banqueting. For the Cynics, such excess was a waste of life and health.

Although neither Jesus nor Luke makes an explicit connection between dropsy and lust for wealth, in the context of this larger passage the connections are clearly there. Jesus' healing of the man with dropsy anticipates the transformation of another man's character away from greed to generosity. Jesus demonstrates in this miracle what the rich man will experience in the parable of the Great Banquet that Jesus will tell while dining at the Pharisee's house.

Two separate encounters, both of which take place during the Pharisee's dinner party, follow the healing of the man with dropsy. In the first encounter Jesus notices a general clamour among the guests for the seats of honour around the table (Luke 14:7-11). Since one's position at the table indicated to other diners one's honour, seating was all-important. Jesus proposes an alternative approach. Rather than fighting for the place of honour, he suggests, guests should willingly take a lesser seat. In doing so, there is a good chance they will be invited to a better place at the table.

However, if they are moved to a lower place, they will be dishonoured. "For," Jesus concludes, "all who exalt themselves will be humbled, and those who humble themselves will be exalted" (14:11). He encourages people to stop seeing meals as times for competition and self-promotion.

Jesus' second encounter at this banquet, this time with his host (14:12-24) has a similar theme. Banquets were considered to be the time to invite (and impress) friends, family and rich neighbours. Jesus says that the normal pattern must be reversed for those who wish to enter the kingdom of God: disciples of Jesus should be inviting outcasts to meals, even though they do not bring the host honour and status. In the parable of the Great Banquet, the host is clearly of high social standing, as are the three people who decline his invitation. All three offer weak excuses, snubbing the one who invited them; he is dishonoured by their refusal to attend his banquet.

The host makes a quick and radical decision to invite another type of guest: the poor, the crippled, the blind, the lame, the homeless. By inviting such people, the host has broken ranks with his peers (the elite). He has dishonoured himself deliberately and irrevocably. Like the man with dropsy who is cured of his insatiable desire for more fluids, the man in the parable is cured of his insatiable desire for more wealth and status.

It takes courage to make a break like this, but this is the kind of courage and faith required of those who follow Jesus. Today we are increasingly susceptible to our consumer culture. Marketing schemes and advertising campaigns are designed precisely to make us feel that, no matter how much we have, we somehow need the thing they are selling! As Christians, we look to Jesus to heal us of this "dropsy," this endless thirst for more, that plagues us.

# 18

# The Samaritan Leper

"Were not ten made clean?"
Luke 17:11-19

For Jesus there is little difference between physical, social and spiritual healing: they go hand in hand. However, in the case of the healing of the 10 lepers, only one is healed on every level and receives the full blessing of God. The story serves as a warning to those who would seek out Jesus only for the physical and social benefits, and quickly forget the spiritual relationship that is established through the healing.

The story opens with Jesus travelling "through the region between Samaria and Galilee" (Luke 17:11). This statement is a bit odd, since the border between these two areas runs east-west and Jesus is, according to Luke, on his way to Jerusalem, to the south. Although commentators often charge Luke with being incorrect in placing Jesus here, a more likely explanation is that Jesus is walking towards Jerusalem along the Jordan River, with Samaria to the west and Perea to the east. Since Perea is under the jurisdiction of Herod Antipas, as is Galilee, Luke considers Perea to be part of a larger designation of "Galilee."

Entering an unnamed village, Jesus encounters 10 lepers who keep their distance from him. As we noted in Chapter 4, the term "leprosy" in the Bible refers to any kind of skin disease or disfiguration. People with leprosy were thought to be "unclean," both physically and spiritually, and were forced to leave the village and live outside the gates. Because any contact with a leprous person would pollute a healthy person, Luke says that the lepers kept their distance from Jesus. However, instead of crying out the usual warning, "Unclean, unclean," signalling people to keep away, these 10 cry in unison, "Jesus, Master, have mercy on us!" (17:13).

Jesus does indeed have mercy on them. He sends them away to show themselves to the priests. In their leprous condition, their doing so would only enrage the priests, who would run the risk of contamination. In this case, the lepers' obedient response to Jesus' command results in their being healed as they make their way to the priests. The role of the priests then becomes important in reintegrating the ex-lepers into the social life of the community. According to Leviticus 14:2-4:

> This shall be the ritual for the leprous person at the time of his cleansing: He shall be brought to the priest; the priest shall go out of the camp, and the priest shall make an examination. If the disease is healed in the leprous person, the priest shall command that two living clean birds and cedarwood and crimson yarn and hyssop be brought for the one who is to be cleansed.

After the requisite sacrifices, the person is allowed a probationary period in the village, and then undergoes ritual cleansings and undertakes more sacrifices. The ritual culminates with the priest making a sin offering "to make atonement for the one to be cleansed from his uncleanness" (Leviticus 14:19). Thus, in the First Testament the healing of leprosy is linked to social and spiritual healing.

In the case of Jesus healing the 10 lepers, the evidence for the "leprosy" disappears en route to the priests. Although all the lepers must have realized that the miraculous cure originated with Jesus, only one returned immediately to thank him. The others were, presumably, more concerned with adding social healing to their now clean physical state. Luke notes that the one who returns was a Samaritan, a fact that Jesus also points to when he calls him a "foreigner." Jews of the first century CE hated the Samaritans. In Jewish eyes, the Samaritans were "half-breeds." Their history went back to the time of the first temple, when Israel was divided between the north and the south. When the northern tribes were invaded and defeated by the Assyrian army in 722 BCE, the Assyrians deported many of the Israelites and imported to the area people of various ethnic backgrounds. Eventually the Israelite tribes disappeared and their territory became populated by an ethnically mixed people – the Samaritans. The Samaritans held on to many of the Israelite traditions but the two remaining southern tribes of

Israel rejected them. Eventually, the Samaritans set up their own temple on Mount Gerizim.

Because of the deep animosity between the Jews and the Samaritans, the priests probably would not have acknowledged the existence of the Samaritan leper, never mind his now non-leprous state. In the eyes of the priests, being a Samaritan would be enough to pollute one for life. Ironically, it is only this man who experiences the fullness of healing that God offers. While the others are cleansed of their disease and, following the priestly rituals laid out in Leviticus, relieved of their social status as outcasts, only this one man is given the pronouncement of Jesus that "your faith has made you well" (Luke 17:19). The English translation disguises the full import of the Greek text, which is literally translated as "Your faith has saved you." In contrast to the other nine, who are "washed," this one grateful supplicant is "saved."

God's grace is given to us freely. However, we should never take that grace for granted. Whenever we suffer illness, it is perhaps understandable that we should turn inward, giving all of our attention and energy to becoming well. But as we heal it is too easy to slip back into old routines, forgetting to give praise and thanks to the One who stands by us in our time of disease and distress. Although our cures may not always be miraculous, God is with us throughout our ordeal. By praising and thanking God for good health we not only become "clean" but also experience the fullness of God's salvation.

# 19

# A Blind-Mute Demoniac

"The kingdom of God has come to you."
Matthew 12:22-28

Once again, one of Jesus' miracles quickly moves him into a controversial dialogue with the Pharisees. There are three movements in this miracle story, each of which centres on a question posed – a question of identity, a question of authority and a question of reality. A different set of characters poses each question, and all of the questions are aimed at the central message of Jesus' miracles: "The kingdom of God has come to you" (Matthew 12:28).

The miracle itself is brief and devoid of details. A man who has lost his hearing and his sight is brought to Jesus. In this case, the root cause of the man's ailments is named – they are caused by demons. Although it would be assumed that all illnesses were caused by an other-worldly spirit of some sort, here it is explicit. The miracle itself is noted with the perfunctory "and he cured him" (v. 22). It is the crowd that poses the first question, a question of identity: "Can this be the Son of David?" (v. 23). The question ascribes to Jesus one of the many titles given to the long-awaited Messiah. In overcoming evil in such a way, the crowd wonders, can Jesus be the one predicted by the prophets and anticipated for generations?

In contrast to the crowd, the Pharisees pose their own question by suggesting that it is not a matter of Jesus' identity but a matter of by whose authority he acts. They think they know the answer: "It is only by Beelzebul, the ruler of the demons, that this fellow casts out the demons" (12:24). A man with the power that Jesus shows must have access to beings fairly high up in the divine hierarchy. In drawing their conclusion, the Pharisees use the name "Beelzebul," or "Baal the Prince," an old Canaanite term that identifies the opponent of God. But no matter what name he goes by – Beelzebul, the Devil, Satan, Lucifer, Prince of Darkness – this evil being stands opposed to the Creator God and is the origin of lies, sin, suffering, sickness and death. In linking Jesus with this evil being, the Pharisees seek to besmirch Jesus' reputation.

Discerning their thinking, Jesus addresses them by pointing to the dilemma that such logic creates: "If Satan casts out Satan, he is divided against himself; how then will his kingdom stand?" (12:26). Jesus and his audience would have been familiar with divisions within a house bringing down an entire kingdom. The triumph of the Maccabean war of the mid-second century BCE had given the Jewish people autonomy in their homeland for the first time in centuries. However, as that century unfolded, the power of the Hasmonean dynasty was whittled away by the infighting over legitimacy of claims to the throne and to the high priesthood of the temple. The result was the entrance of the Romans under Pompey in 63 BCE. Eventually, the Romans declared Herod the Great "king" over all the land. However, Herod's paranoia over factions within his own household led to the division of his kingdom after his death, with the largest share eventually falling under the control of a Roman governor (Pontius Pilate held this post during Jesus' ministry).

The truth of Jesus' statement about Satan casting out Satan needed no illustration. If demons and unclean spirits were assumed to be the ultimate cause behind every sickness and disease (as was the prevailing belief), then casting them out through the power of their master, Satan, would serve no purpose. Just as Herod's dynasty eventually crumbled from internal strife, pitting himself against his own minions would only serve to undermine Satan's power.

As if to drive home the illogic of the Pharisees' position, Jesus turns their accusation on them. In the first century CE, stories circulated of other Jewish exorcists who were known to have been active among the people of Israel, exorcists such as Abraham,[7] David,[8] Solomon[9] and Tobias (Tobit 6:1-18; 7:15–8:9). Josephus even recounts that Eleazar the Pharisee was an exorcist, although he dates to after Jesus' time.[10] Jesus rightly points out that if the power to do such miracles lies with Satan, then the Pharisees accuse not only Jesus himself but all the Jewish exorcists before and after him. Such a sweeping accusation, suggests Jesus, will be repaid with the witness of the exorcists against the Pharisees themselves.

Having demolished the Pharisees' argument, Jesus proposes his own alternative. If it is not through the power of Satan that Jesus acts, perhaps there is another explanation – he acts by the Spirit of God. In the divine hierarchy as it was understood in antiquity, the effects of a spirit being such as demon could only be countered through an appeal to a more powerful divine being. If this being was not Satan, the highest in the hierarchy of evil beings, then it must be the opponent of Satan. Indeed, it is God who stands against the evil that afflicts the sick and possessed.

In proposing this alternative, Jesus reframes the question. It is not a question of authority but a question of reality. If the Spirit of God is now active in such a powerful and public way, something in the world has changed. God does not look on from afar, indifferent to the plight of human beings. God has entered into the world to take an active part in combatting evil. Satan's kingdom is not divided against itself; Satan's kingdom is at war with God. And Jesus intends to help God win!

The forces of evil are active in our age, as they have been throughout the ages of humankind. As Christians we stand opposed to evil wherever and in whatever form we find it. We live to reveal the in-breaking of God into our world. However,

Jesus' argument has profound implications for Christian resistance to evil. If it is true that Satan cannot oppose himself lest his whole empire of evil crumble, the same is true for Christians. If in the name of God Christians argue and fight, slinging accusations at and opposing one another, how can the kingdom of God stand in this world? "Every kingdom divided against itself is laid waste," says Jesus (v. 25). This must also be true for the kingdom of God. As Christians we are responsible for working towards unity and harmony in our common witness that the kingdom of God has entered this world.

# 20

## A Coin Found in a Fish

"The children are free."
Matthew 17:24-27

This odd little miracle is one of only two places in the Gospels where the issue of taxation is raised in Jesus' ministry. The other is the question of paying taxes to Caesar that the Pharisees pose to Jesus (Matthew 22:15-22).

In the first century CE, over 90 per cent of the population of Palestine lived in rural villages. The people were very poor. The majority did not own the land they worked but leased it from the wealthy aristocracy. Much of their profits from the land was sent to Jerusalem, where most of the landowners lived, to pay their lease. To make matters worse, a triple tax burden was imposed on the people: the religious taxes, such as the temple tax, tithes and offerings, which were sent to Jerusalem; the Herodian tax, instituted by Herod the Great and continued by his successors to support their massive building projects throughout the land; and the Roman tax, which financed such things such as roads, aqueducts and policing. This "tribute tax" served as a reminder of the occupation and was often enforced by the military. People also had to pay other indirect taxes, such as the collection of tolls for the transport of goods, import/export duties and market taxes.

The Jerusalem elite often subcontracted the collection of taxes. There were three levels of tax collectors, each of whom took a cut of the intake. The Jerusalem rulers and aristocracy held the right to collect specific taxes. District chief tax collectors were supervisory officials who purchased the right to oversee a specific area. They paid the tax assessment in advance and then organized the collection in their district in the hope of turning a profit. It was risky, but some managed to become rich. Others collected the taxes at tollbooths or tax offices after bidding on the right to collect taxes locally. To meet the requirements of the authorities, each level added a bit to the required tax to turn a bigger profit.

Because of the heavy taxes, people were constantly in debt and on the edge of destitution. Some lost inherited family land and eventually fell into debt-slavery if they could not pay. Peasants saw most of their money going to the minority elite in Jerusalem. When they needed to borrow money they had to borrow it from these same people, and pay it back with interest, further indebting themselves and increasing the wealth of the elite. It is no wonder, then, that many of the Jewish nationalists, bandits and rebels in the first century CE saw in the taxation system a symbol of their oppression. There was much resentment among the people towards the priestly aristocracy of

Jerusalem as well as towards the Romans, but little could be done about it.

In the Western world today, goods, including money, are thought to be unlimited. If there is a shortage of something we can either produce more or redistribute from where there is a surplus. If a person acquires more goods, we do not assume it has been taken from someone else. We hold to a theory of an ever-expanding economy with a generally well-off middle class. There are plenty of people in a state of comfort who are unwilling to disrupt the status quo.

This was not the case in antiquity, where wealth was thought to be of a limited quantity. All goods existed in a limited, finite supply that was already distributed. By analogy we might think of a pie: it can be sliced in many different ways, but ultimately there is only so much pie to go around. If one person gained more wealth, it would be assumed that the money had been taken away from someone else. The pie never grew larger; there was no expanding economy. If everything was distributed properly, then everyone would have what they needed. In this view, hoarding of riches constituted social injustice. Poverty meant not only that one had been dealt an injustice somewhere along the way, but also that one was powerless to change things. To be labelled "rich" was not just an economic statement but a social and moral one.

In the Second Testament, the question of taxation becomes a question of justice. Due to the oppressive practices of the elite, into whose hands the taxes eventually fell, there was little hope that wealth would be redistributed to the poor people. Tax collectors were regarded with disdain – note their constant association with sinners in Second Testament texts. Nevertheless, Jesus chooses to include such persons among his social acquaintances, even making one of them a disciple (Levi, the tax collector). Not surprisingly, Jesus' opponents question his views on taxation. To the Pharisees, who were *not* among the Jerusalem elite, Jesus must have seemed very much like a friend to those who perpetuated the cycle of poverty for so many.

When Jesus arrives in Jerusalem shortly before he is put to death, some of the elite challenge him directly on this issue: "Is it lawful to pay taxes to the emperor, or not?" (Matthew 22:17). He manages to avoid the question by revealing their hypocrisy in carrying a coin that bears the image of the Emperor. However, in the coin in the mouth of a fish episode, which took place earlier in Galilee, Jesus shows how the prevailing understanding that goods are limited is at odds with the view that God's kingdom is breaking into this world.

After Peter affirms Jesus' practice of paying the temple tax when challenged by some Pharisees, Jesus turns it into an object lesson. He points out that the rulers of the world do not tax their own family. (For example, the families of the Emperor and of Herod were exempt from paying taxes.) Rather, those who are not related to rulers are taxed. The temple tax was a half-shekel annual payment Jewish men had to make to help maintain the temple. For Jesus, being a child of the God who created the heavens and the earth means being free from paying a tax in order to worship that same God. As part of the family of God one is exempt, since God is available everywhere and at all times.

Nevertheless, Jesus decides that in this case it is more expedient to pay the tax. His action here should not be taken as affirming an oppressive taxation system. Throughout his ministry Jesus opposes the exploitation of people. But here, paying the temple tax avoids an altercation that could escalate into a civic arrest, as the Romans did not take kindly to a person who refused to pay taxes, no matter what kind of tax it was.

The miraculous nature of the appearance of the coin in a fish shows that taxes are of no consequence for Jesus. The funds do not come out of his pocket. More significantly, the appearance of the coin in a fish, in part of the created order, undermines the cultural notion of limited goods. How can it be that a fish has received part of the pie? Jesus shows that God can create money from nothing.

With the in-breaking of the kingdom of God, the old order that sees a concentration of wealth in the hands of the few will be overturned as God provides for those who have nothing. Peter's object lesson becomes a paradigm for our own Christian discipleship as we seek to ensure that all of God's creation has equal access to the resources that are available. We are called to dismantle the obstacles that would see wealth concentrated in the hands of the few at the expense of the many. If everything belongs to the kingdom of God, then nothing can be claimed as ours alone.

# 21

# Changing Water into Wine

"What concern is that to you and to me?"
John 2:1-11

In this first of the seven "signs" in John's Gospel, Jesus travels to a wedding in the small village of Cana, 15 kilometres (9 miles) northwest of his hometown, Nazareth. As Jesus, his mother and his disciples have all been invited, it is likely that a relative or close associate (perhaps even a relative of the disciple Nathanael, who was from Cana – see John 21:2) is being married. In the first century, a wedding party could span a few days, often ending only when the food and wine ran out. The length of the party reflected the honour of the host: the longer the party, the wealthier the host. The practice of serving the best wine before the inferior wine (v. 10) was the usual custom at social gatherings; this ensured that the guests appreciated the better vintage before becoming too inebriated.

When the wine runs out, Mary points out the situation to Jesus, saying, "They have no wine" (v. 3). Although many people read Mary's comment as a request for Jesus to perform a miracle, nothing in the text itself suggests that Mary expected him to do so. Although it might be argued that she knows of his abilities from past experience, including the miraculous conception of Jesus, nothing in John's narrative indicates that Jesus is expected to perform a miracle. Indeed, if Mary is requesting a miracle, Jesus' response to her request is odd: "Woman, what concern is that to you and to me?" (2:4). There is some debate over whether Jesus' use of the word "woman" for his mother is a solemn and respectful address or a rebuke. A similarly toned address is used in Mark's Gospel when demons disrespectfully challenge Jesus, saying, "What have you to do with us, Jesus of Nazareth?" (Mark 1:24; in the original Greek text, the wording of the phrase is almost identical: literally, "what [is it] to me/us and you?"). Thus, it does seem likely that Jesus' response to his mother is a mild rebuke.

If Jesus is rebuking his mother for asking for a miracle, it seems strange that he would then carry out a miracle, seemingly fixing the very problem she has identified. Despite our reluctance to see Jesus speaking harshly to his mother, the fact that Jesus is fickle, in one instance rejecting the request for a miracle and in the next performing one, is also disturbing.

A simpler explanation, and one that avoids these problems, is to understand Mary's comment as letting Jesus know that the party is over; it is time to go home. She knows this because the wine has run out. Jesus' response, "My hour has not yet come" (John 2:4), would then be understood as Jesus saying, "But it's not time to go!" The harsh tone of his voice in his first response, "Woman, what concern is that to you and to me?" indicates that Mary has overstepped a cultural boundary in announcing to Jesus that it is time to leave. In the absence of his father, Jesus would be the eldest male blood relative of Mary present and thus would, in that culture, be the one who would decide when to leave. Mary then turns to the host's household slaves and tells them to do whatever Jesus tells them (2:5). Presumably they are there because Mary asked them to come along and pack up the donkey for the trip home. Realizing she has overstepped her boundaries, she now submits to Jesus' authority.

Jesus' statement "My hour has not yet come" has a double meaning. On the surface, it simply means that it is not time to leave the party. However, on a deeper level, it suggests that Jesus' anticipated hour of glory, manifest through the cross and resurrection, is not yet upon him. This latter sense of "my hour" becomes clearer in subsequent passages (see John 4:21, 23; 5:25; 8:20; 12:23, 27-28; 13:1; 17:1). Turning to the household slaves, Jesus commands them to fill the six large water jars. (I doubt they would have been pleased with the task, as each jar could hold 136 litres [180 gallons] of water!) Likely other guests have realized that the wine has run out and are beginning to look for the slaves to help them pack up to leave.

Our narrator, John, tells the reader in an aside that the jars that Jesus directed the slaves to fill were not the empty wine jars but rather the stone water jars reserved for use in the Jewish rite of purification. It is likely that John realizes in this "sign" an echo of Moses changing water to blood in the Egyptians' stone jars (Exodus 7:19). Indeed, this comparison will become more apparent later when John links the eucharistic elements of bread and wine to the life given through Jesus: "Those who eat my flesh and drink my blood have eternal life" (John 6:53). Rather than the previous rite of purification, which comes through water, for Christians the means to sanctification is through the wine that is the blood of Jesus.

The result of this miracle for the people present at the wedding is rather low-key. Clearly, Jesus was not concerned about receiving recognition for his miracle; he lets the steward's remark to the bridegroom about having "kept the good wine until now" pass without comment (John 2:9-10). For the reader of the Gospel, however, there is an implication that Jesus himself is the "best wine" that has been kept for the end and is now manifest. Only the household slaves and Jesus' disciples seem to be aware that a miracle has happened at all. The final comment, that "His disciples believed in him" (2:11), suggests that before this incident, they were unsure of Jesus' identity even though they had chosen to follow him.

The miracle at Cana reveals the glory of Jesus (2:11) by showing his power over the natural world. The turning of water into wine indicates the presence of the divine within Jesus and therefore within the world. However, there are other equally important lessons to be learned from this miracle. Unlike the miracles in the Synoptic Gospels, which tend to attract crowds or enrage opponents, this "sign" is subtle. Jesus reveals who he is to his closest friends while meeting the immediate needs of others at the wedding, particularly the bridegroom, whose celebration seems threatened by the shortage of wine. As we think about our own Christian faith and how we share it, we need to be aware that there are many ways to proclaim Jesus. While in some instances it might be appropriate to win over a crowd or engage in debate, at other times subtlety and kindness are more important testimonies to the glory of the Lord.

# 22

# The Royal Official's Son

"Sir, come down before my little boy dies."
John 4:46-54

This second miracle, or "sign," in John's Gospel is clearly connected to the first. Both are associated with the small Galilean village of Cana and both conclude with the narrator stating that they are signs. In the opening verse, the narrator reminds us of the previous miracle since, in the interim, Jesus has travelled to Jerusalem to perform the symbolic cleansing of the temple, had a clandestine meeting with the Pharisee Nicodemus, had a theological discussion with the followers of John the Baptist, and brought to belief a woman of Samaria and her entire village. Geographically, Jesus has come full circle.

There are differences between the two miracles. Although Jesus is in Cana, the ill boy is in Capernaum, some 30 kilometres (18 miles) away. The walk between the two villages was easily done in a day, although the official seems to have lingered overnight in Cana (as the roadside meeting between the official and his slaves on the day after his meeting with Jesus shows – see John

4:52). Despite his son's illness, the father was willing to be away from his home for at least a day or two in order to seek out a miraculous cure for the boy. The distance the official travelled could be construed as a testimony to the man's faith, but it more likely represents his desperation.

During the time of Jesus' ministry, many Roman troops were garrisoned in Galilee; one might assume that the unnamed royal official was part of the Roman administration, if one considers the similarity between this miracle and the healing of the centurion's slave (Matthew 8:5-13; Luke 7:1-10). However, Herod Antipas, the son of Herod the Great, oversaw the administration of Galilee, appointing a number of royal administrative officials to the region. It is likely that this official worked for Herod Antipas, since the Greek word used to describe him is from the root for "king." Thus, the man who comes to Jesus is a representative of the very political ruler who opposes Jesus and his Galilean ministry.

Jesus rebuffs the official's first approach by turning to the crowd around him, saying, "Unless you see signs and wonders you will not believe" (John 4:48; the pronoun "you" is plural in Greek). Implicit in the comment is a hint of condemnation. People should not need signs and wonders in order to believe. Much later in John's Gospel Jesus notes to Thomas, who demands evidence for Jesus' resurrection, "Blessed are those who have not seen and yet have come to believe" (John 20:29). Although Jesus performs signs and wonders, strong faith is not to be grounded in such things.

Indeed, the royal official himself protests to make his intentions clear. He is not requesting a sign in order to authenticate Jesus' relationship to God. Rather, his request grows out of personal desperation in the face of a life-or-death situation: "Sir, come down before my little boy dies" (John 4:49).

A number of similarities exist between this healing miracle and the healing of the centurion's slave in the Synoptic Gospels (Matthew 8:5-13; Luke 7:1-10). In the Synoptic story, the centurion and Jesus are both in Capernaum when the request for healing is made. When Jesus offers to come to his house the centurion refuses him with words that indicate his prior belief in Jesus' abilities: "Lord, I am not worthy to have you come under my roof; but only speak the word, and my servant will be healed" (Matthew 8:8). Upon hearing the centurion's confession of faith in Jesus' ability to heal the slave, Jesus makes his pronouncement: "Truly I tell you, in no one in Israel have I found such faith" (8:10). In the miracle story in John, it is not until the official hears these words from Jesus that he believes. His belief is later justified when on his return trip to Capernaum he receives the news of his son's recovery. At this second point he is again said to have "believed," this time in Jesus himself rather than in Jesus' ability to do miracles.

His whole household is said to come to believe in Jesus at this point as well. In antiquity, the household – which included the eldest male, his wife and children, perhaps his mother, sisters, younger brothers and their families, and slaves –

was the basic building block of society, especially in rural villages. If the head of the household (*paterfamilias*) decided to adopt new beliefs, as seems to be the case here, all others in the household would be required to follow his lead.

It is interesting to note that like the first sign in John's Gospel, where Jesus turns water into wine, this miracle has a fairly small audience, and only a few people are said to come to believe in Jesus as a result. Nevertheless, in selecting the miracles to recount, John chose these two over other more spectacular public miracles of Jesus. This choice reflects John's concern about people who believe in Jesus for the wrong reasons. John is careful to have us understand that these miracles are "signs" and therefore point beyond themselves to the one who performs them. From John's point of view, a belief in Jesus grounded only in his miracles is inadequate. True faith in Jesus looks beyond the signs to the sign maker. For John, the need for "signs and wonders" is contrasted with the faith of the Samaritans whom Jesus visited prior to this point in the Gospel (John 4:39-42). The Samaritans come to believe in Jesus on the basis of his words (John 4:41), not his signs.

Today many people continue to look to God for signs and wonders, demanding that God perform miracles so they can truly believe. Although demanding empirical proof before making a commitment is an understandable human need, particularly in a scientific era, this is not true faith in Jesus. While the signs and wonders themselves are not problematic, and can often deepen faith, it is the *demand* for signs and wonders that proves troublesome. As the royal official came to Jesus in a time of desperation, so can we turn to God in our desperate times. However, to demand that God perform at our convenience will incur Jesus' disdainful reply: "Unless you see signs and wonders you will not believe" (John 4:48).

# 23

# Healing the Paralyzed Man

"Do you want to be made well?"
John 5:1-18

In the miracle stories of the Synoptic Gospels, the crowds generally respond favourably to Jesus' miracles. Although there are occasions when they side with the Pharisees, for the most part they tend not to stand in Jesus' way. It is only after he enters Jerusalem that the Jewish leaders seek to have him killed, although it is the priests rather than the Pharisees who plot against him (Mark 11:18). In John, those seeking to kill Jesus surface earlier in the narrative and span the spectrum of Jewish leadership groups. The plot against Jesus' life begins as a result of this third miracle that he performs (John 5:18).

Immediately following the healing of the royal official's son in Galilee, Jesus returns to Jerusalem to attend another festival. During Jesus' time there were three Jewish festivals that required travel to Jerusalem: Passover, Pentecost and Tabernacles. Since Jesus was last in Jerusalem for Passover, this feast is probably Pentecost. When Jesus sees a paralyzed man by a pool in the city, he immediately gains insight into the man's plight. For 38 years the man has been unable to walk. Given that the average age of a man in the first century was 40, it is likely that the man has not walked for most of his life; Jesus knows that the man has been waiting at the pool for a long time. In verse 9 we learn that the man was lying upon a mat. The word translated as "mat" indicates a pallet or mattress used by the poor. Thus, along with being sick, the man is, not surprisingly, poor. What is more, we learn, he has no friends, no doubt because he is poor and sick.

Depending on the version of the Bible one uses, verse 4 may or may not be included in the story. This verse records how an angel stirs up the pool water at certain times of the year, which gives the pool healing properties for the first person who goes in. In the NRSV Bible, this verse is relegated to the footnotes as it was probably not in the story as John wrote it (it is missing from the earliest and best manuscripts). In all likelihood, a scribe added the verse to explain the sick man's lament: "I have no one to put me into the pool when the water is stirred up" (v. 7). Because he is ill, the man needs friends or family to help him, but he has none.

Unlike the situation in many of the Synoptic healing miracles, here Jesus is not approached on behalf of the man but takes the initiative himself. The critical element of faith, either that of the sick person or of friends and relatives, is absent from this account. Jesus walks over to the man and asks him, "Do you want to be made well?" (v. 6). The man seems to misunderstand Jesus' intentions and responds to Jesus by explaining why he has never been the first one to enter the stirred water. It seems from his response that he does not know Jesus and is not aware of Jesus' powers. Rather than explain himself, Jesus senses that the answer to the question is a resounding "yes," and he commands the man to stand up and walk, which he does. The man expresses no faith, except faith in the healing powers of the pool water.

In the ensuing confusion, while the man is coming to terms with his new-found ability to walk, Jesus slips away. At this point the controversy begins. On his way through the city, "the Jews" stop the man and inform him that he is breaking Sabbath law: "It is not lawful for you to carry your mat" (v. 10). They are only doing their job, and are right when they say that this action is forbidden. In his own defence, the man repeats the command of Jesus, pointing also to his miraculous healing. Rather than being calmed by his explanation, "the Jews" are incensed to learn of someone healing on the Sabbath.

At this point, we must pause for a moment to explore the identity of "the Jews" in John's Gospel. I deliberately use quotation marks around the designation to remind us that they are literary characters in John's story. As such, they are caricatures of a broad range of individuals. By the time John writes his Gospel, some 50 years have passed since the death of Jesus. In the meantime, the temple has been destroyed, most Jewish groups have been broken up, and those that remain are seeking to solidify their collective identity. As part of that process, there seems to have been an attempt to push Jewish believers in Jesus out of the synagogues. This is a fate that has befallen some in John's community, and they are not pleased about it.

In telling the story of Jesus, the later Christians project their frustration with the Jewish leaders of their day onto Jesus' day. Rather than carefully designating Pharisees or Sadducees as opponents of Jesus, they lump all opponents of Jesus together under the term "the Jews." It is a sad fact of Christian history that such language has been used to justify the persecution of Jews in general, when in reality it reflects an inter-Jewish debate over the legitimate claim on that identity. Thus, when we read of "the Jews" opposing Jesus we need to remind ourselves that these men are not representative of Jews everywhere; they are literary characters that help John make his point.

Let us return to the healing of the paralyzed man. The cross-examination of the man by "the Jews" does not lead them to the identity of Jesus. However, later that day Jesus seeks out the man to warn him not to sin lest he should fall ill once again. Although Jesus consistently eschews the prevailing cultural notion that illness is a direct result of sin, in this case he uses that same notion to instill in the man the fear of God. It could be that this man needs to develop a fear of God, as he has not expressed faith in Jesus even after being healed.

This lack of faith in or awareness of Jesus is an important part of the next stage of the narrative. Not knowing that he could create a conflict between Jesus and the Jewish leaders, the man returns to the latter to report that he has discovered the identity of his healer. The conflict escalates when Jesus, in his meeting with the leaders, justifies his action by noting his familial connection with God: "My Father is still working, and I also am working" (John 5:17). At this point, the authorities lose sight of the miracle and see only Jesus' breaking of Sabbath law and his blasphemy. Some say that their accusation against Jesus is that he is attempting to be like God, as Adam did (Genesis 3:5-6). Others suggest that the background lies in the Greco-Roman legends of certain men who were thought to have gained divinity by doing heroic "labours" or works, the best-known example being Heracles (the Roman Hercules). Although Jesus does not perform miracles in order to become divine, his opponents think this is what he is trying to do. For Jesus, however, the basis of his identity is grounded in his relationship with God: "I can do nothing on my own" (John 5:30).

Like the Judean leaders in the story who refuse to acknowledge this miracle and its significance, many people today refuse to acknowledge the work of God in the lives of others. Rather than listen to the testimony of the person who is in relationship with God, they choose to make accusations. Nevertheless, we are not called to judge these accusers. Rather, we are called to have confidence in our relationship with God and to seek out those who require our help, as Jesus did. Neither lack of praise nor abundance of opposition should prevent us from ministering to those in need.

# 24

# Feeding the Many

"Sir, give us this bread always."
John 6:1-14, 25-35

As this narrative opens, we find that the miraculous healing that Jesus is bringing to the sick has attracted a large crowd. While some in the crowd might themselves need healing, the majority seem to be drawn to Jesus because of the signs he is performing. They are, for the most part, the poor of society, as shown by the type of bread the boy produces later in the story. Although wheat bread was most common in antiquity, barley loaves were cheaper and thus were the staple of the poor. The people are living in an occupied land, with little hope for the future, and Jesus is bringing to them a glimpse of the kingdom of God.

Unlike the previous three signs in John's Gospel, this miracle has a large audience. Although John implies that there have been other public miracles, this is the first one in which the crowd's reaction will be narrated. The scene is set on a hillside by the Sea of Galilee. The crowd gathering around Jesus is large and hungry, and Jesus asks the obvious question: "Where are we to buy bread for these people to eat?" (v. 5). It turns out that this is a test of the disciple Philip's faith in Jesus' ability, for the narrator tells us that Jesus knew what he was going to do. Unlike the crowd, Philip has seen Jesus act when faced with a shortage, for he was at Cana when Jesus turned the water into wine. The disciples do not make the connection, and one of them merely points to a little boy who has nothing but five barley loaves and two fish. Although this amount of bread and fish would be a banquet for the boy and his family, it would not go far in a crowd of 5,000.

When the disciple Andrew points out the boy with the fish and bread, he probably does not intend to suggest that the boy's provisions should be distributed among the crowd. His point seems rather to be that a collective picnic was not likely among the folks gathered there. Although some may have bits and pieces of a meal, the boy's simple fare shows that it will not be enough for everyone. Jesus takes this paltry amount and extends it throughout the entire crowd so that all have their fill, with some to spare. His action is reminiscent of the prophet Elisha, who takes 20 barley loaves and fresh ears of grain from a man and, at the command of God, give them to a hundred people. When his servant resists, Elisha declares, "Give it to the people and let them eat, for thus says the LORD, 'They shall eat and have some left'" (2 Kings 4:42). The servant does as he is commanded and sure enough, after the people have eaten, they have some left "according to the word of the LORD" (2 Kings 4:44). This allusion to

Elisha shows Jesus to be even greater than the great First Testament prophet. No wonder the crowd seeks to "take him by force to make him king" (6:15).

Before Jesus distributes the loaves and fish he gives thanks over them (John 6:11). The Greek word for "give thanks" is *euchariste*. From its root we get the word "Eucharist." The word itself has no particular Christian, or even religious, meaning. It simply indicates thanks. However, it took on significance in the Christian faith early on as it came to be attached to Jesus' institution of the Lord's Supper. These echoes of the Eucharist raise an important issue. It may surprise some readers to learn that the Gospel of John contains no account of the Last Supper that Jesus shared with his disciples. Although he enters into a private and lengthy discourse with the twelve, there is no institution of the Eucharist in John's narrative.

In light of this absence of an account of the Lord's Supper, many commentators suggest that the multiplying of the loaves and fish, along with the changing of water into wine (John 2:1-11), function in John as replacements for the account – a Eucharist on a grand scale! In support of this theory, they point to a second- or third-century CE fresco in the Alexandrian catacomb that joins the symbolism from the two miracles (bread, fish and wine). A few early Christian writers also make the connection, suggesting an early affiliation between the two miracles in John and the Eucharist. The care with which Jesus directs his disciples to gather up the fragments might reflect the reverence with which the eucharistic elements came to be regarded.

Lest anyone think this too far-fetched, let us jump ahead a bit in the narrative. At the conclusion of the meal, Jesus realizes that the crowd intends to take him by force and make him king, so he withdraws into the hillside (John 6:15). That evening, he joins his disciples in the boat on the Sea of Galilee and crosses with them to the other side (the walking on water miracle occurs here, which we shall discuss in the next chapter). It is only when the crowds catch up to Jesus the next day that he explains to them the significance of the multiplying of the loaves and fish.

The crowd does not seek out Jesus because they have faith in him. They seek him out because they have experienced a sign. The crowd makes the connection between bread from heaven and the manna given to the Israelites during their wanderings (6:31, cf. Exodus 16). However, Jesus is quick to correct their misunderstanding of the story, which emphasizes the manna provided by Moses: "Very truly, I tell you, it was not Moses who gave you the bread from heaven, but it is my Father who gives you the true bread from heaven" (6:32). It is this latter bread that "comes down from heaven and gives life to the world" (6:33). Upon hearing this, the crowd demands, "Sir, give us this bread always" (6:34). Jesus responds, "I am the bread of life" (6:35). As the manna was life for those wandering in the desert, so Jesus is at the heart of the spiritual life for Christians. The warning comes later in the narrative, when Jesus explains:

"Very truly, I tell you, unless you eat the flesh of the Son of Man and drink his blood, you have no life in you. Those who eat my flesh and drink my blood have eternal life, and I will raise them up on the last day; for my flesh is true food and my blood is true drink. Those who eat my flesh and drink my blood abide in me, and I in them" (John 6:53-56).

Thus, we see that Jesus makes an explicit connection between this feeding miracle and the consumption of the elements of the Eucharist as a remembrance of Jesus' presence among God's people.

All too often we as Christians respond to the issues of overpopulation and world hunger in the same way Philip and Andrew respond to Jesus, questioning our ability to even begin to address the problem (6:7-9). However, the miracles show us that we must not respond to such situations with despair. Rather, we are called to do what we can with the little we have, even in the face of the overwhelming needs of the people. It may be a matter of supplying a little food, as the boy did, or carrying out the work of redistribution in the name of Jesus. If we really believe that Jesus is the bread of life, each of us needs to ask what we might do individually to address the needs of the hungry in our world. As the elements of the Eucharist sustain us in our spiritual life, our contributions, however meagre, may sustain others in their physical life.

# 25

## Walking on Water

"It is I; do not be afraid."
John 6:15-21

In the midst of the miracle of the multiplying of
the loaves and fish and the discussion with the
crowd that it provokes, the disciples alone witness
another miracle of Jesus. It begins when Jesus
retreats to the mountains to escape the crowd,
which wishes to make him king. Having experienced the feeding of the 5,000, they take it as a
sign that Jesus is the long-awaited Messiah, come
to restore the kingdom of Israel. Although they are
correct in thinking Jesus is the Messiah, it is not
Jesus' intention to reinstate Israel through violent
action.

The disciples finally tire of waiting for Jesus.
Knowing the dangers of travelling across the Sea
of Galilee at any time of day, they leave at dusk,
before it gets too late. As fishermen, they are aware
that strong winds can arise in the south and race
up the Jordan River valley, instantly turning the
calm sea into a violent tempest. Nevertheless, one
might wonder how they imagined Jesus would
catch up with them, since there was only one boat

on the shore (John 6:22). Certainly they were not expecting Jesus to walk on the water, as is indicated by their response to seeing him – "They were terrified" (v. 19).

Jesus' response in the face of their terror is, "It is I; do not be afraid" (6:20). The opening Greek phrase might more literally be translated as "*I* am," with an emphasis on the personal pronoun. This is one of a series of Jesus' statements in John's Gospel that are referred to as "I am" sayings. In seven places, the phrase "I am" is followed by a metaphor describing a characteristic of Jesus: "I am the bread of life" (6:35; cf. vv. 41, 48, 51); "I am the light of the world" (8:12; 9:5); "I am the gate [for the sheep]" (10:7, 9); "I am the good shepherd" (10:11, 14); "I am the resurrection and the life" (11:25); "I am the way, and the truth, and the life" (14:6); "I am the true vine" (15:1, 5). The emphasis is not on the "I" but on the metaphor, which describes Jesus' relationship to others: Jesus is the source of eternal life (life, resurrection); Jesus is the means through whom others find life (way, gate); Jesus leads others to life (shepherd); Jesus reveals to others the truth (truth); Jesus nourishes their life (bread, vine). In these functions, Jesus acts as God acts. The symbolism of the First Testament that describes God's relationship to Israel (particularly bread, light, shepherd and vine) is applied to Jesus. He functions as God does throughout the history of Israel.

In each of these "I am" sayings, Jesus draws on a metaphor to explain his identity. More significant, however, are the few occasions where the phrase "I am" stands alone in an absolute sense, where there is no metaphor attached. Most significant is Jesus' statement "Very truly, I tell you, before Abraham was, I am" (John 8:58). Grammatically, the phrase "I am" must be regarded as complete and meaningful in itself. The response of "the Jews" provides the conclusive point: "They picked up stones to throw at him" (8:59). They are presented as understanding Jesus to be making divine claims. In chapter 13 of John's Gospel, Jesus tells the disciples about their mission of service and Judas' imminent betrayal of him, saying, "I tell you this now, before it occurs, so that when it does occur, you may believe that I am he" (John 13:19). In this statement, the phrase "I am" is presented as an object of belief.

In order to understand the full import of this claim, and the reason "the Jews" reacted as they did in chapter 8 of John, we must turn to the First Testament. Exodus 3:14 is the primary text from which we draw our understanding of the divine name. It is known as the Tetragrammaton because it consists of four letters: YHWH. It is customary to expand these letters into the name Yahweh, although this represents only an educated guess concerning the original spelling and pronunciation of the word. In Exodus 3:14, the name YHWH is connected with the verb form "I am," which is understood as a proper name and is repeated three times: "I am who I am," and "I am has sent…." It is a difficult phrase to translate, but it shows the claim of "I am" to be linked with claims to divinity.

We see this again in the Greek version of Isaiah 52:6, which can be translated as "My people shall know my name; in that day [they shall know] that 'I am' is the one who speaks." The phrase "I am" becomes the divine name to be known in the Day of the Lord. When Jesus uses the absolute sense of "I am," it has clear implications for his identity. Jesus not only applies divine attributes to himself by using metaphors, he also uses the divine name ("I am") for himself. Jesus and the LORD are one and the same. In announcing himself as "I am" to the disciples in the boat, Jesus is making a statement about his divinity.

Strengthening this suggestion is the link between Jesus' walking on water and the acts of God in the First Testament. Besides the obvious connection with the miracle of Israel crossing over the Red Sea in Exodus 14:21-22, other First Testament passages provide important background for understanding the full import of Jesus' miracle. Psalm 77 praises God with the words "Your way was through the sea, your path, through the mighty waters; yet your footprints were unseen" (v. 19). Psalm 107 recounts how sailors were caught in a storm and cast about on the sea: "Then they cried to the LORD in their trouble, and he brought them out from their distress; he made the storm be still, and the waves of the sea were hushed" (vv. 28-29). In John 6:15-21, Jesus approaches the disciples in the boat by walking on the water, despite the storm. He calms the disciples' fear by assuring them with the words "I am." In so doing, he uses an expression that makes clear claims to divinity. It would remind them of the God of the First Testament, whose power over nature was supreme.

As with the miracle of the calming of the storm (see Chapter 7 of this book), the boat in this miracle story is frequently compared to the Church, and the disciples to modern Christians. We might want to explore further details of the story in light of such an allegory by asking ourselves about the storms that can arise in a Church that forgets to include Jesus as its focus. How can refocusing on Jesus (taking him "into the boat") help to calm some of the storms and fears in the Church?

# 26

# Healing the Blind Man

"Do you also want to become his disciples?"
John 9:1-41

The healing of the blind man reflects the themes of the Gospel of John as a whole. In the prologue to the Gospel John writes: "The true light, which enlightens everyone, was coming into the world" (John 1:9). His own people did not accept the presence of the light, but to those who did receive him "he gave power to become children of God" (v. 12). This receiving of light, leading to becoming a child of God, is illustrated through the story of the blind man in chapter 9 of John. Jesus, the light of the world (John 8:12), gives sight to a man born to darkness.

In the encounter, the blind man receives his physical sight from Jesus immediately. As the story progresses, the blind man gradually receives spiritual insight as well, while the blindness of the Pharisees is revealed. There is a progression in the blind man's coming to true faith in Jesus. At each stage, the blind man makes a statement about Jesus' identity: "the man," "a prophet," "from God," "Lord." Although they oppose Jesus and seek to discredit the man, the Pharisees in the story actually help the man come to faith by giving him the opportunity to reflect on Jesus' identity.

There are seven scenes in the chapter, each of which is primarily an interchange between two characters or groups of characters: Jesus, the blind man, his neighbours, his parents and the Pharisees. The story opens with the healing of the blind man (John 9:1-7). As they enter a village, the disciples notice the man and ask a difficult theological question: "Rabbi, who sinned, this man or his parents, that he was born blind?" (9:2). It is a valid question. The prevailing assumption was that God caused illness, often as a punishment for one's sin. However, if a person was born with an ailment, he or she could not have sinned in order to deserve the punishment; it must have been the parents' sin. If this were the case, one could then question the justice of the punishment. Jesus' response is to highlight the false dichotomy in the disciples' question. The man was blind "that God's works might be revealed in him" (v. 3). As a result of his obedience to Jesus' command to wash in the pool of Siloam, the blind man gains his sight.

The second section of the narrative focuses on the blind man and his neighbours (9:8-12). The neighbours wonder whether this is the same man who used to beg by the gate. Some say, "It is he," while others say, "No, but it is someone like him." Ironically, both responses are true. It is the man who used to beg, but he is no longer the same man. When they confront him and he confirms his identity they demand to know how he is now able to see. The man born blind tells them, describing Jesus as "a man." He is not yet fully aware of Jesus' true identity.

In the third section, the (formerly) blind man appears before the Pharisees, who question him about Jesus (9:13-17). Some of the Pharisees think Jesus is not from God because he broke the Sabbath. Even if one argued that healing was not a sin on the Sabbath, Jesus' use of a paste of clay and spit was deliberately provocative. The mixing of paste was expressly forbidden on the Sabbath, and we know from other miracles that Jesus did not need to use it for his power to be effective. The Pharisees' own debate, and their questioning of the man who had been healed, provoke the man towards a deeper understanding of Jesus' identity. Realizing that in order to perform such a sign Jesus must be more than "a man," he declares Jesus to be a prophet.

The fourth and central scene of the story is the encounter between the Pharisees and the man's parents (9:18-23). When the scene opens, it seems the Pharisees who supported Jesus have quietly left; only those who oppose him remain. Rather than attack the healing on the Sabbath, they now deny that it took place and call before them the man's parents. The author is clear that the parents fear they will be expelled from the synagogue and will not confess an opinion of Jesus' identity. Their reticence speaks to the Jewish Christians in John's community who are unwilling to confess Jesus as the Messiah. By showing the parents to be ridiculous, John shows his own readers how ridiculous they are if they deny Jesus.

The next scene returns us to the blind man and the Pharisees (9:24-34). Having failed in their attempt to have the man implicate Jesus in the breaking of the Sabbath, they now make the accusation themselves: "Give glory to God! We know that this man is a sinner" (9:24). The opening phrase is usually an admonition to honesty, but here it is used to advocate a falsehood. In demanding that the man tell the truth, they utter a falsehood. Their continued pressing of the man causes him to ask, "Do you also want to become his disciples?" (v. 27). Of course the reader knows that not only are they not interested in discipleship, they are, in fact, intent on killing Jesus. Their intimidation tactics do not work because the man stands his ground, pointing to Jesus' ability to heal as an indication that he is not only a prophet, but a prophet "from God" (9:33). In their frustration, the Pharisees cast the man out of the synagogue, charging that he was "born entirely in sin" (v. 34). This is a clear reference to the disciples' question at the opening of the story, and the Pharisees' charge is more ridiculous in light of the fact that the man can now see.

The second-last scene has Jesus coming to the man again (9:35-38). Jesus asks the man whether he believes in the Son of Man. The formerly blind man says, "And who is he, sir?" using a Greek term of formal address, *kyrie* ("Sir"). Jesus' next response brings to the fore the healing of the man's condition: "You have seen him, and the one speaking with you is he" (9:37). The man now comes to full belief in Jesus, saying, "Lord, I believe." Here the Greek word *kyrie* ("Lord") is used again, but this time with divine implications, as the man's action of worshipping Jesus shows. The man has now gained not only his physical sight but also spiritual insight into the identity of Jesus.

In the final scene, Jesus and the Pharisees come face to face (9:39-41). When Jesus says, "I came into this world for judgment so that those who do not see may see, and those who do see may become blind" (9:39), he alludes to the Pharisees' blindness. He agrees with them that they are not blind, and as such they are guilty of sin (they "see" the truth about Jesus but refuse to recognize him). Unlike the blind man, who sought to do something about his condition on both the physical and the spiritual level, the Pharisees claim not to need the spiritual insight Jesus brings.

We see in this story the stages by which the blind man develops faith in Jesus. Despite a number of challenges and obstacles from his neighbours, his parents and especially the Pharisees, the blind man gradually comes to the awareness that the person who healed him is more than a man, more than a prophet, more than a person sent from God. Jesus is the Lord. Unlike many others who experience Jesus' healing as a result of their faith, this man experiences faith as a result of the healing. Compare your own experience of coming to faith in Jesus with that of the blind man. How did it begin? What obstacles have you encountered? Has your faith grown and developed? Reflecting on our own experiences of faith in Christ can help us know how to present our faith to our friends and neighbours.

# 27

# The Raising of Lazarus

"Lord, he whom you love is ill."
John 11:1-46


In our age, there is an almost sacred aura around a hospital. It is a place of life and death, new birth and old age, rejoicing and mourning, hope and fear. The place of the hospital in our modern life reflects an unspoken credo of our culture: "This life is all there is; it must be preserved at all costs." It is a credo that most of us, Christians included, would affirm – if not in principle, then in practice. Our society denies the reality of death, even though we live with this reality all the time. Doctors and nurses work hard to keep people alive, yet all of us will die eventually.

Even in the process of death, we fight hard to stay alive and to keep others alive through life-support systems and radical interventions and treatments. Life is prolonged as long as possible – and who would want it otherwise? Even in death, we preserve the depiction of life. At funeral homes we visit open caskets where people have been preserved to look as if they are merely asleep.

There is nothing good in death – for those who die, or for those who are left behind. Christianity affirms that death is not God's ideal. Paul calls death the last enemy to be destroyed (1 Corinthians 15:26).

When we read the story of the raising of Lazarus, we need to be clear that death is viewed negatively. The death of Lazarus, as with the death of anyone, forces us to face our own fears, our own mortality. Jesus raises Lazarus not to indicate that we can escape death – for we cannot – but to underline our appreciation for the life we now have. This is not a story of life beyond the grave; it is a story of life *without* the grave.

One of the more difficult verses in this story is the shortest verse in the Bible: "Jesus began to weep" (John 11:35). Those in the crowd observing Jesus think he is weeping because the one he loves has died. In fact, there is much debate among biblical commentators over why Jesus is weeping. Because Lazarus is dead? Because the mourners do not understand his message of resurrection? I think Jesus weeps because he is angry at death. This is the sense of his emotions in verse 33: he is "greatly disturbed in spirit and deeply moved." Quite literally, Jesus was "moved with indignation in spirit," that is, "angry." From the very creation of the world, death was not intended. In the Garden of Eden, life was eternal. God's presence was to be enjoyed, but so were the fruits of the earth. It was only when sin entered into the world that this ideal broke down. With disobedience and sin came death. Life could no longer be enjoyed without the fear and worry of death.

Nevertheless, death does reveal God. Upon hearing about Lazarus' death Jesus responds enigmatically: "This illness does not lead to death; rather it is for God's glory, so that the Son of God may be glorified through it" (John 11:4). The words "glory" and "glorified" are not used in the sense of "praise" or "honour." Rather, they are used in the sense of "revelation." Lazarus' death has happened in order to reveal God and the Son of God. They are revealed for who they are: the authors of life. It is not that God made Lazarus terminally ill as some great object lesson. Rather, illness and death are made to serve God's larger scheme of things.

Similar things happen today. Often it is only through an illness or a close encounter with death, or even in the face of death itself, that one comes to acknowledge God. There are countless stories of deathbed conversions to God, but very few stories of the denial of faith. People certainly experience anger and fear upon finding out they are ill. But for many, facing illness or death forces them to reflect on that which is beyond this life.

We see this idea in Jesus' words to the disciples: "Lazarus is dead. For your sake I am glad I was not there, so that you may believe" (11:14-15). But the disciples do not understand and think that going to Judea will result in Jesus' death. The irony is that Jesus is not going there in order to die, but to bring back life; and yet he will later die in Judea and as a result bring life everlasting. For now, Jesus sees

Lazarus' death as a means to strengthen the disciples' faith.

At the same time, death is not the final word. When Jesus hears that Lazarus is sick, he tarries for two days before heading towards the village of Bethany. He then suggests that he and the disciples return to Judea. Based on past experience, the disciples know what to expect. They remind Jesus that some were seeking to kill him (John 11:8). This statement is not news to Jesus, for Jesus knows that his death is inevitable, although not as the disciples imagine it. Until then, he must carry on with his ministry while he can. This is the meaning of his saying in verses 9-10:

> "Are there not twelve hours of daylight? Those who walk during the day do not stumble, because they see the light of this world. But those who walk at night stumble, because the light is not in them."

Light and life are joined in Jesus' sayings. Thus, those who walk in light walk as if they live, not as if they are dying. Those who walk "in the valley of the shadow of death," in darkness, do not experience life.

Clearly the story of the raising of Lazarus has some connection with Jesus' death and resurrection. Yet there are significant differences between Jesus and Lazarus: Lazarus is still wrapped up in the grave clothes when he exits the tomb; Lazarus does not receive a new body but rather the body he had before he died; and Lazarus returns healthy, but not immune to disease, death and decay. He will die again. In contrast, Jesus' resurrection is a one-time event that brings about eternal life for all of us. Lazarus' resurrection points towards an affirmation of this life. We are to enjoy the good things God gives us and help others to do so. Yet, Jesus' words in verses 25-26 call into question the modern emphasis on preserving life at all costs: "I am the resurrection and the life. Those who believe in me, even though they die, will live, and everyone who lives and believes in me will never die."

As Christians we know that even when medical interventions fail and life slips away, death is not the end. Jesus has conquered death and offers us the promise of the eternal life. Death is overcome. Let us live as if we believe this to be true! Alleluia!

# Notes

[1]   Josephus, *War of the Jews* 8:46-49.

[2]   John L. McLaughlin, *The Questions of Jesus* (Ottawa:
      Novalis, 2001), 17-18.

[3]   Willi Braun, *Feasting and Social Rhetoric in Luke 14*
      (Cambridge, UK: Cambridge University Press, 1995),
      esp. 22-131.

[4]   Stobaeus

[5]   *Epode* 2.2.146-9.

[6]   *Fasti* 1.215-16.

[7]   Qumran, *Genesis Apocryphon* 20.8-34.

[8]   Josephus, *Antiquities* 6.166-69.

[9]   Josephus, *Antiquities* 8.44-45.

[10]  Josephus, *Antiquities* 8.46-49.

# Index of Scripture References

*Genesis*
3:5-6      132

*Exodus*
3:2      82
3:6      82
3:10      82
3:11      82
3:14      82, 140
4:3      82
4:6-8      84
4:10-17      84
5:22-6:9      84
6:28-7:5      84
7:19      121
15-      13
14:21-22      141
16      136
20:8-11      44
20:13      46
22:27      46

*Leviticus*
13:45-46      34
14:2-4      104
14:19      105
15:19      60
15:25-30      60
19:18      46
19:19      95-96
24:17      46
24:21      46
25      89

*Numbers*
12:9-12      37
35:16-31      46

*Deuteronomy*
5:12-15      45
6:4      46
22:9-11      96

*Judges*
3:12-14      93
3:15      93
6:12      82
6:13      83
6:14      83
6:15      83
6:17-24      83
6:36-40      84
10:7-8      93
10:8      94
11:1-33      94

*1 Kings*
12      94
15:1      94
15:4      94
17:8-16      89
17:8-24      88

*2 Kings*
2:11      88
4:42      134
4:44      134
5:1-14      89
5:14      35
5:27      37

| | |
|---|---|
| 15:15 | 37 |
| 23:22 | 94 |
| 23:24 | 94 |

*2 Chronicles*
| | |
|---|---|
| 26:19-23 | 37 |

*Psalm*
| | |
|---|---|
| 77:19 | 141 |
| 107:28-29 | 141 |

*Isaiah*
| | |
|---|---|
| 20:1-6 | 78 |
| 35:5-6 | 70 |
| 36-37 | 13 |
| 52:6 | 140 |

*Jeremiah*
| | |
|---|---|
| 7:11 | 79 |
| 19:1-13 | 78 |
| 32:1 | 94 |
| 32:6 | 95 |
| 33:14-15 | 95 |

*Ezekiel*
| | |
|---|---|
| 5:1-4 | 78 |

*Hosea*
| | |
|---|---|
| 1:2-3 | 78 |

*Zechariah*
| | |
|---|---|
| 14:21 | 79 |

*Tobit*
| | |
|---|---|
| 6:1-18 | 109 |
| 7:15-8:9 | 109 |

*Wisdom of Solomon*
| | |
|---|---|
| 2:24 | 14 |

*Matthew*
| | |
|---|---|
| 5:17 | 45 |
| 8:5-13 | 124, 125 |
| 8:8 | 125 |
| 8:10 | 125 |
| 8:25 | 49 |
| 8:28 | 53 |
| 12:22-28 | 107-111 |
| 15:22 | 64 |
| 15:23 | 64 |
| 15:28 | 66 |
| 17:15 | 71 |
| 17:24-27 | 112-117 |
| 21:19 | 77 |
| 22:15-22 | 112 |
| 22:17 | 115 |

*Mark*
| | |
|---|---|
| 1:1 | 27, 68 |
| 1:15 | 13 |
| 1:16-20 | 32 |
| 1:21-28 | 24-28 |
| 1:23-26 | 54 |
| 1:24 | 119 |
| 1:25 | 31 |
| 1:29-31 | 29-33 |
| 1:32-34 | 19-23 |
| 1:34 | 11 |
| 1:35 | 32 |
| 1:36 | 32 |
| 1:40-45 | 34-38 |
| 2:1-12 | 39-42 |
| 2:27-28 | 44 |
| 3:1-6 | 43-47 |
| 3:4 | 45 |
| 4:35-41 | 48-52 |
| 5:1-20 | 53-57 |
| 5:21-42 | 58-62 |

| | | | |
|---|---|---|---|
| 7:24-30 | 63-66, 89 | 9:28-36 | 88 |
| 7:31 | 63 | 9:38 | 72 |
| 7:32-37 | 67 | 11:38 | 97 |
| 8:18 | 69 | 13:1-4 | 91 |
| 8:18 | 50 | 13:4 | 93 |
| 8:22-26 | 67-70 | 13:10-17 | 91-96 |
| 8:23-27 | 50 | 13:18-19 | 95 |
| 8:26 | 51 | 13:16 | 20 |
| 8:27-30 | 68 | 14:1-24 | 97-102 |
| 8:29 | 27, 68 | 14:7-11 | 97 |
| 8:31 | 68, 69 | 14:12-14 | 97 |
| 9:14-29 | 71-75 | 15:2 | 97 |
| 9:30-32 | 68 | 17:7-8 | 97 |
| 10:32-34 | 68 | 17:11-19 | |
| 11:12-14 | 76-80 | | |
| 11:15-19 | 77 | *John* | |
| 11:18 | 128 | 1:9 | 143 |
| 11:20-25 | 76-80 | 1:12 | 143 |
| 11:25 | 80 | 2:1-11 | 118-122 |
| 12:29-31 | 46 | 2:11 | 22 |
| | | 4:21,23 | 120 |
| *Luke* | | 4:39-42 | 126 |
| 4:17-21 | 89 | 4:46-54 | 123-127 |
| 4:25-26 | 89 | 4:54 | 22 |
| 4:18 | 21 | 5:1-18 | 128-132 |
| 4:38-39 | 31 | 5:25 | 120 |
| 4:40 | 31 | 5:30 | 132 |
| 4:35 | 31 | 6:1-14 | 133-137 |
| 5:1-11 | 81-85 | 6:14 | 22 |
| 6:4 | 97 | 6:15-21 | 138-142 |
| 7:1-10 | 124, 125 | 6:25-35 | 133-137 |
| 7:11-17 | 86-90 | 6:35 | 139 |
| 7:38 | 97 | 6:41 | 139 |
| 7:49 | 97 | 6:48 | 139 |
| 7:44 | 97 | 6:51 | 139 |
| 7:49 | 97 | 6:53 | 120 |
| 8:26 | 53 | 6:53-56 | 137 |
| 8:30 | 55 | 8:12 | 139, 143 |
| 9:19 | 86 | 8:20 | 120 |

| | | | |
|---|---|---|---|
| 8:58 | 140 | *Acts* | |
| 8:59 | 140 | 6:1 | 90 |
| 9:1-41 | 143 | | |
| 9:5 | 139 | *Romans* | |
| 9:16 | 22 | 2:12 | 14 |
| 9:39 | 147 | 13:9 | 46 |
| 9:39-41 | 147 | *1 Corinthians* | |
| 10:7 | 139 | 15:26 | 149 |
| 10:9 | 139 | | |
| 10:11 | 139 | *Galatians* | |
| 10:14 | 139 | 5:14 | 46 |
| 11:1-46 | 148-152 | *Philippians* | |
| 11:25 | 139 | 3:10-14 | 85 |
| 11:45 | 22 | | |
| 12:18 | 22 | *1 Thessalonians* | |
| 12:23 | 120 | 5:17 | 75 |
| 12:27-28 | 120 | *James* | |
| 13:1 | 120 | 2:8 | 46 |
| 13:19 | 140 | | |
| 14:6 | 139 | *Revelation* | |
| 15:1 | 139 | 13:18 | 93 |
| 15:5 | 139 | | |
| 17:1 | 120 | | |
| 20:29 | 124 | | |
| 21:1-11 | 48 | | |
| 21:2 | 118 | | |
| 21:25 | 50 | | |

# Appendix

## Synopsis Chart of Jesus' Miracles

| Miracle | Mark | Matthew | Luke | John |
|---|---|---|---|---|
| Jesus the Miracle Worker | 1:32-34 | 8:16-17 | 4:40-41 | |
| The Synagogue Demoniac | 1:21-28 | | 4:31-37 | |
| Simon Peter's Mother-in-Law | 1:29-31 | 8:14-15 | 4:38-39 | |
| A Man with Leprosy | 1:40-45 | 8:1-4 | 5:12-16 | |
| The Paralyzed Man | 2:1-12 | 9:2-8 | 5:18-26 | |
| A Man with a Withered Hand | 3:1-6 | 12:9-13 | 6:6-10 | |
| Calming the Storm | 4:35-41 | 8:23-27 | 8:22-25 | |
| The Gerasene Demoniac | 5:1-20 | 8:28-34 | 8:26-39 | |
| The Woman with a Hemorrhage | 5:21-42 | 9:18-26 | 8:40-56 | |
| The Gentile Woman's Daughter | 7:24-30 | 15:21-28 | | |
| The Blind Man at Bethsaida | 8:22-26 | | | |
| The Spirit-Possessed Boy | 9:14-29 | 17:14-21 | 9:37-43 | |
| The Withering of the Fig Tree | 11:12-25 | 21:18-22 | | |
| The Large Catch of Fish | | | 5:1-11 | (21:1-11) |
| Resuscitating a Widows' Son | | | 7:11-17 | |
| The Bent-over Woman | | | 13:10-17 | |
| The Man with Dropsy | | | 14:1-4 | |
| The Samaritan Leper | | | 17:11-19 | |
| A Blind-Mute Demoniac | (3:19b-22) | 12:22-24 | 11:14-16 | |
| A Coin Found in a Fish | | 17:24-27 | | |
| Changing Water Into Wine | | | | 2:1-11 |
| The Royal Official's Son | | (8:5-13) | (7:1-10) | 4:46-54 |
| Healing the Paralyzed Man | | | | 5:1-18 |
| Feeding the Many | 6:34-44 | 14:14-21 | 9:12-17 | 6:1-14 |
| Walking on Water | 6:45-52 | 14:22-33 | | 6:15-21 |
| Healing the Blind Man | | | | 9:1-41 |
| The Raising of Lazarus | | | | 11:1-46 |

# Also available from Novalis

The Questions of Jesus
*John L. McLaughlin*

Available in 2004
Parables of Jesus

Available in 2005
Teachings of Jesus

For these and other
fine books, contact
NOVALIS
1-877-702-7773
or
cservice@novalis.ca